the meaning of

TANGO

The Story of the Argentinian Dance

Christine Denniston   **PORTICO**

This edition published in the United Kingdom in 2015 by
Portico
43 Great Ormond Street
London
WC1N 3HZ

An imprint of Pavilion Books Company Ltd

ISBN 978-1-90603-216-6

A CIP catalogue record for this book is available from the British Library.

10 9 8 7 6

Printed and bound by Imak Ofset, Turkey.

This book can be ordered direct from the publisher at www.pavilionbooks.com

CONTENTS

FOREWORD
by Gloria and Eduardo Arquimbau

The Tango has existed for between 130 and 150 years. In that time it has had two periods of great worldwide success.

The first was towards the beginning of the twentieth century, long enough ago to mean that none of us had the opportunity to experience it first-hand. But we Tango lovers know what Tango was like then because we can listen to recordings on 78rpm discs, some of which have now been made available on CDs, and because we can read books written by people who were there. These are the things that help what we love survive into the future.

The second worldwide success of Tango was the result of the show *Tango Argentino*. The show was first performed in Europe in 1983, was a hit on Broadway in 1985, and then took the Tango around the entire world. We can talk about this from our own experience as performers in the show, which dazzled the whole world. We also know it was the spark that motivated people everywhere to dance the Tango. People approached the dancers in the show asking us to teach them Tango the way it was danced in Argentina, and this was the reason that, at the junction of the streets Corrientes and Esmeralda in Buenos Aires, we opened our Tango school called Volver ('to return').

It was here that we taught our first Tango students, and it was here that we first met Christine Denniston, who came to visit us each time she came to Buenos Aires to study the Tango. She learned and absorbed a great deal about the dance, and about the history of Tango.

Since those days we have maintained our friendship and stayed in contact. When we travel to London to teach or perform she is always with us, not only translating for us, but also taking us to visit the major venues that hosted the great Tango orchestras of the early twentieth century.

We think it is very important that she records in a book her understanding of Tango, as a woman, as a dancer, as a teacher and as a researcher. We are sure, from our friendship and our many talks about Tango, that we will feel ourselves dancing on every page of this book.

We repeat: These are the things that help what we love survive into the future.

Buenos Aires, 2007

Gloria and Eduardo Arquimbau are currently the longest established professional Tango couple in the world. They first met in the mid-1950s when Eduardo was already gaining a reputation as a Tango dancer, and cemented their professional relationship in 1960. They pioneered Tango choreography on television, becoming the face of Tango for a generation of Argentinians. They have travelled the world, not only as members of the company of Tango Argentino, but also with their own shows, and have performed with almost all of the great Tango orchestras of the Golden Age.

INTRODUCTION

When I first fell in love with the Tango, my aim was simply to make myself as nice to dance with as I possibly could, so that good dancers would want to dance with me.

I was very fortunate that I stumbled across a group of people who were determined to understand how Tango was danced in Buenos Aires. To begin with we took classes where we could, and shared the little information that we had. Often we found that the things different people told us about the Tango were contradictory and confusing. There was only one thing to do, and that was to go to Buenos Aires and find out how it was really done.

Buenos Aires is a magical city, where no matter how busy a person is they are never so busy that they don't have three hours for a quick cup of coffee, where the sun shines and the sky is blue almost every day, where the streets are lined with grand, elegant buildings, and where even a boiled potato tastes better than you could ever have expected. It is a place where every visitor starts planning their next trip before they leave.

Over many visits to Buenos Aires, always searching for the dancers who were nicest to dance with so that I could make myself most like them, I slowly realised that there was far more to know about Tango than I could have begun to imagine when I first started.

Most importantly, I discovered that the confusing and contradictory things that people had told me in the early part of my search hid a simple truth – the people I most enjoyed dancing with all danced in the same way. And I was not alone. Everyone I knew most enjoyed dancing with people who danced this way.

That is not to say that they all did the same steps – far from it! The richness and variety of Tango is one of its most extraordinary characteristics. But the reason that I could dance with any of these people, even when they led steps that I had never seen before, was that fundamentally they were all speaking the same language. Some chose to speak it simply, others created complex poetry with our feet, but once I had learned the language I could understand them all.

I also discovered that many of the people who danced in this way were people who had learned to dance the Tango in Buenos Aires in the 1940s and 1950s – in the Golden Age of Tango. (Tango historians usually define the Golden Age of Tango as the period between 1935 and 1955, though some would start it a decade earlier.) There certainly were people in the new generation of Tango dancers who danced the same way, but amongst the older generation this way of dancing was the norm. At first I thought it was a matter of experience – that people who had been dancing a long time had simply had more practice – but as I began really to understand what the dancers were doing, I realised that it was not just that many of the younger dancers were doing the same dance less skilfully. Some of them were doing the same steps, but they were doing them in a different way – so different that it started to feel almost like a different dance.

That seems less surprising when looked at in the context of Argentinian history in general, as well as the history of Tango in particular. For various reasons that I shall try to explain, practically no one learned to dance the Tango between 1955 and 1983. When a new generation came to Tango in the 1980s and 1990s, at the start of the Tango

Renaissance, the social realities of Buenos Aires, and the practical realities of how a person learned to dance, had changed.

All living things evolve, and it is natural that any creative form will change over time. A problem arises, though, when there is a discontinuity and a whole generation does not learn the form. There is a risk that an entire culture will be lost.

Many languages have been lost in this way in the last century. The common pattern is that a generation of children is educated in the language of an economically or politically dominant power, using that language in their daily life instead of their parents' language, and then the following generation does not learn to speak the language of their grandparents at all. The language will only survive if a new generation learns to speak it fluently while there are still native speakers of the language alive. Otherwise a unique culture will disappear.

Tango in the 1950s had a richness unparalleled in any other social dance I have ever experienced. Dancers who danced at that time contained within their bodies the distilled wisdom of a hundred years of evolution and development. Then, quite suddenly, a generation simply did not learn to dance the Tango at all.

In the mid-1990s I realised that we had already lost many of the great dancers of the 1940s and 1950s, who carried in their bodies the wisdom of all the generations who had danced before them. Each time another dancer died, irreplaceable knowledge died with him or her. It seemed to me important that as much knowledge as possible be saved before it was gone forever. That was the reason I went to live in Buenos Aires in 1996. I wanted to absorb as much knowledge as my body could hold.

It is not possible for one person to know everything there is to know about Tango. Tango in the Golden Age was too large and too rich for any one person to absorb it all. Another person spending time in Buenos Aires might have had a completely different experience dancing with different people in different milongas. I can only pass on the knowledge that I have.

My own personal experience of the Tango Renaissance goes back to 1992. When I talk about the beginning of the Tango Renaissance, and about the Golden Age of Tango, I am relying on the experience of a wide range of friends, acquaintances and teachers. Many of these were people I got to know well, so that I had an understanding not just of the literal meaning of their words, but the deeper meaning behind them, and the personal stories that shaped them. I hoped that by combining the widest picture I could get of the general experience with the deepest picture I could discover of individual experiences, I could start to comprehend the truth of what Tango really is and was. Among the dear friends with whom I spent countless happy hours dancing and talking were people who had started to dance as early as 1940, almost at the beginning of the Golden Age, so when I talk about Tango between 1940 and the early 1990s I am sharing my understanding of the experiences they shared with me.

I did have some opportunities to talk to a small number of people who danced in the 1930s, or even a little earlier, though not as many as I would have liked. I have tried to base my comments on Tango before 1940 on the evidence that survives from the period, wherever possible, rather than on the recollections of the few people I spoke to who were there, or on the memories of others about what they had been told by the previous generation. I have done my best to study that available evidence, and to sift out the real information about Tango, leaving behind comments that are misleading or inaccurate, hoping that the experience of Tango I bring to the research helps me to do that in a way that is useful. Again, someone else going back to these same sources may come to a different conclusion.

I have tried not to comment on things for which I feel there is insufficient real evidence to draw a solid conclusion. This includes the earliest history of Tango. There are a variety of theories about the earliest beginnings of Tango, some of them passionately held. I shall attempt to give a few relevant facts, and try to resist the temptation to draw conclusions.

I shall talk frequently about Buenos Aires and the Tango. Tango is an urban phenomenon, and in Argentina it was Buenos Aires that danced the Tango. In the rest of the country the most popular dances were the ones usually classed together by Argentinians under the name 'Folklore' (not 'folklore' in the sense in which we use the word in English).

Across the borders of the city of Buenos Aires, in the Greater Buenos Aires area, Tango certainly was danced. My experience of Tango as danced by those who learned outside the city was that, though similar, their technique was different in some very important respects. I chose to concentrate my own research on the dancers who danced with the technique of the city itself (though some lived across the city borders), as this technique seemed to be the one that, to my taste at least, gave consistently the best experience of the dance.

For much of the history of Tango, Buenos Aires and Montevideo, capital of Uruguay, were twin cities sharing a culture. We know that many important Tango musicians and poets were born in Uruguay, and that many prominent Argentinian musicians travelled to Uruguay to play for dancers. Tango should properly be thought of not simply as 'Argentinian', but as 'Rioplatense' – coming from the area around the Rio de la Plata. I do not discuss Tango in Uruguay because in my own trips to Uruguay I failed to find dancers who had been dancing in the Golden Age, or in the years when the social dance had been forced underground in Buenos Aires. I found only people who had started to dance as part of the Tango Renaissance. This means that I have no personal knowledge of the history of Tango in Uruguay, or of how the Uruguayans understood Tango. Montevideo is a much smaller city than Buenos Aires, and this probably explains why even in the 1990s there were not enough dancers from the 1940s and 1950s left to influence the new Tango scene there. But it is important to note that Uruguay was Tango's other home and second mother.

My own experience of Tango in Buenos Aires was one of receiving amazing generosity from wonderful people who had learned to dance in the 1940s and 1950s. It was as though, once they saw my desire to understand the dance they loved, they tore their heart from their body to give it to me, and I shall never be able fully to express my gratitude to them. They longed for their dance to be passed on to a new generation, and were afraid that it would be lost forever. Whenever they met someone who wanted to learn they poured out their knowledge, desperate for other people to learn and remember what they knew.

Many of my dear friends in Buenos Aires have gone now. That generation is almost completely lost to us. A new generation of Tango dancers is growing up, in Buenos Aires and around the world, that has never had the opportunity to dance with people who danced the Tango in its Golden Age. It is up to those of us who did dance with them, who benefited from their generosity, to do what we can to pass on what the Tango meant to them. This book is my attempt to record their Tango, their gift to me, and is my tribute to them.

A book is an imperfect way of passing on information about a dance. For the sake of brevity and clarity it is necessary to oversimplify some things. Tango generates a great deal of passion, and views are deeply held. There are always those who will disagree with any opinion. And it is impossible to find a way of describing any aspect of Tango technique without saying something that can be misinterpreted. I shall try to do justice to the memory of the dancers who gave me the Tango, and to find words to describe their experience and their dance. I can only hope that they, and my readers, will be charitable when I fail.

Tango is a contagion. The best way to pick it up is through close contact with a heavily infected body. Still, I hope this book will help people who dance the Tango to make an informed choice about how they want to dance. And for those who do not dance, I hope it will give an insight into one of the loveliest flowers of human civilisation, a *flor del fango* – a flower of the mud – which grew in harsh, unpromising circumstances, yet became something uniquely beautiful.

KEY TO THE ILLUSTRATIONS

Leader		Follower
	Position of the body	
	Foot bearing weight	
	Free foot	

The position of the bodies has been shown in all the graphics, as understanding the relationship between the bodies is vital to understanding Tango. Where the position of the feet is important, the feet have also been shown.

The graphics have been shown from above so that the relationship between the bodies is clear. Viewed from above, the dancers' feet would be hidden by the dancer's bodies. In order to make it possible to see where the feet are, the position of the feet has been shown over the position of the bodies.

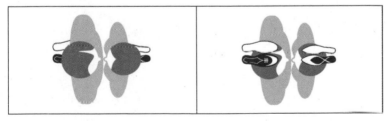

When shown in the correct position the feet are hidden.

With the feet shown over the bodies their position can be seen.

PART 1

THE MEANING AND PURPOSE OF TANGO

UNDERSTANDING TANGO

Imagine a young man at the end of the nineteenth century, fourteen, fifteen or sixteen years old, living in a village with his large extended family in one of the poorest parts of Spain or Italy. He hears that the Argentinian government is running a campaign to bring people just like him to their country. They will find him a place to stay, feed him for the first week he is there, and help him find work. He has already heard that Argentina is one of the richest countries in the world – far richer than his own country – so he decides he will go there, make his fortune, and then come home and build a grand new house for his mother.

The construction of the railways in the middle of the nineteenth century opened up Argentina's huge agricultural and mineral resources, but there was one natural resource that Argentina had a terrible shortage of – people. Even in the late twentieth century the population was less than 40 million in a country over eleven times the size of the United Kingdom. In the nineteenth century this remote corner of the old Spanish Empire was practically deserted.

The government, aware of the need for workers to exploit the natural riches of their country, made a conscious decision to attract immigrants, specifically from Europe. Young Europeans were offered subsidies, free accommodation and free food on arrival, and promised land or work.

The land rarely materialised, and the work was often terribly hard and lonely, in some of the remotest parts of this empty country. But, enchanted by the promises, the immigrants poured in – hundreds of thousands of them every year – and in Buenos Aires they quickly came to outnumber the existing population. Unlike, say, the United States, where it was not unusual for whole families or communities to arrive, maybe fleeing religious or political persecution at home, but certainly planning to stay and start a new life in a new land, in Argentina the immigrants were overwhelmingly single young men who were looking for work, many of whom thought they would get rich and then go home.

Men in Buenos Aires in 1906

So our young man leaves, for the first time in his life, his mother, his sisters, cousins and aunts, and makes the long boat trip to Argentina. He arrives in the great port of Buenos Aires, only a few years earlier practically a village itself, now a bizarre mixture of sophisticated European capital city and Wild West frontier town. There are more people in each street than he has ever seen before in his whole life, and practically all of them are men.

Probably he never did make his fortune, never did build that grand house for his beloved Mama. In fact, he probably never saw his mother again. The hopes and ambitions he had when he began his long journey crumbled. Some made fortunes, of course, and the rich got very, very rich indeed. But the majority remained poor, or got by, or built a little business and did all right for themselves, but never quite got to be rich.

Avenida de Mayo, Buenos Aires, in 1894

Our young man finds himself far from everyone who has ever loved him and everyone he has ever loved. Perhaps in another place he would have consoled himself by getting married, starting a new family, having children to love. But the city he is in is a city of men. Maybe he will be one of the lucky few to find a woman to love him, but the odds are against him. Perhaps, if he makes a little money, he may be able to bring over a mail-order bride. The chances are, though, that he will find himself completely in the company of men.

Some men, of course, are happy in the company of men and feel no need for feminine companionship. For the majority, though, something vital was being denied them. Buenos Aires, especially in the poorer suburbs, was a dangerous place where men carried knives the size of short-swords in their belts. A macho, independent front was a necessity. Anything else was a sign of weakness. Many of the men must have found the loneliness and isolation almost intolerable.

The only place where they could express their softness – the sweet, tender part of their nature – was either in the arms of a prostitute, or dancing the Tango.

The Tango had begun in the middle of the nineteenth century, mixing elements of music and dance brought to Argentina by the many small immigrant communities. It was one of the first dances to use the shocking new hold, popularised by the Viennese Waltz, in which a man and a woman stood in front of each other and put their arms around each other. A true street dance, it was not created by dancers and taught to people, as so many European dances have been. It was thrown together by people who might not have shared a common verbal language, but who wanted to move together to the pretty new music being made around them, and who were searching for a moment of joy in their often hard lives.

To dance with the women in Buenos Aires the immigrants had to learn their dance – and learn to do it in a way that pleased the women, or the women would not dance with them. The unique pressures of this extraordinary city, in this extraordinary moment of its history, formed the evolving Tango, and made it into something more than just a dance. The Tango became an expression of a fundamental human need:

The Hunger of the Soul for Contact with Another Soul

Traditional Methods of Learning the Tango

The Tango was a cornerstone of Argentinian culture. Certainly by the 1940s, and probably long before, there was only one – surprisingly formal – way for a man to learn the dance.

A young man starting to become aware of the charms of young women would also be aware that the only socially acceptable way to meet them was dancing the Tango. And even as late as the 1940s and early 1950s, the peculiar history of Buenos Aires, as well as its social conventions, meant that in the formal dance halls, known as milongas, there were always far more men than women. If a young man went to a milonga with a step or two and a lot of hope, none of the women would dance with him, because the room was full of men who were already skilled dancers. To get a woman into his arms at all, he had to be able to dance, and to dance with the most attractive women and the best dancers, he had to be very good indeed.

To learn how to dance, the young man would go to a men-only practice dance, known as a práctica. He would watch for a while, and then one of the older men would decide to start to teach him how to follow – that is, to dance what is traditionally seen as the woman's role. The novice would be taught the grammar of Tango – the technique that is fundamental to everything – how to stand, how to walk, and how the bodies relate to one another. These are the things that define the dance and make the communication and comprehension between the two dancers possible. He would also begin to pick up a sense of the vocabulary of Tango – the common moves that emerge as a result of the technique, which are the shapes that dress the communication and give it outward form.

Posed photograph of men dancing in 1903

When the young man was considered good enough as a follower, a process that usually took several months of going to the práctica four or five times a week, the older men would invite him to try to lead another young man who was also following well. He would try to lead some of the steps the more experienced men were leading. Sometimes the younger men would be shown steps by the older men. Sometimes they would watch, and then work out the steps together.

Because both the leader and follower were experienced in the grammar of the dance, and had experienced the vocabulary from the follower's side, they could quickly and accurately work out together the best way of combining steps, and of leading them so they could be followed by someone who had never followed that combination of steps before.

One day one of the older men would tell the young man to put on his best suit, because he was going with them to a milonga. Naturally, no woman would dance with him in the milonga unless she had seen him dance and knew that he could do it. So his more experienced companions would ask a woman who was a friend, as a special favour to them, to dance with him, so the others could see.

If his first milonga didn't go well, it would be back to the práctica for a few more months before he dared to try again. Even when he was a success in the milongas, with lots of women wanting to dance with him, he would continue to go to his práctica, to learn more, to create his own steps, and generally to practise dancing both parts. Sometimes in the prácticas two men would give a demonstration dancing together, and the standard was expected to be very high. The standard of general dancing in the prácticas, too, could be outstanding. In the best prácticas it would be higher than in the milongas.

The whole process, from first going to a práctica to first dancing with a woman, generally took a man three years, with the first nine months spent only following.

I asked many men, from many different parts of Buenos Aires, why they decided to start the long process of leaning how to dance the Tango. Almost without exception they would get a faraway look in their eyes, a smile would dart across their face, and they would say, 'There was this girl, you see . . .'

One man, born in the early 1930s, told me that as a child he hated the Tango because his uncles made him sit and wind up their gramophone when they practised at home, while all he wanted to do was go out and play. But a few years later, when the girl he was dreaming of told him he should learn to dance the Tango, he found the best dancer in his part of town and asked him to recommend a práctica. He knew there was no alternative. If he didn't learn how to dance, his chances of ever getting a girlfriend were practically nonexistent. What happened to the girl he never told me, but the love he found for the Tango stayed with him all his life.

The mechanisms for learning the dance for a woman were less structured. Generally women learned in the home from their fathers or brothers, or from their mothers or sisters. Women's experience of leading was one of the better-kept secrets of the Tango. However, while there was no public forum for women to dance together, they did practise together in private. The first time a woman who had danced in the Golden Age told me she had learned by dancing with her mother, she was very amused by the look of surprise on my face. I had been under the impression that in the Golden Age women did not lead, but the fact was that her mother had been a skilled leader. To her this was quite normal.

The process of learning for the novice was the same as for a man learning to follow. She would be trained in the technique of the dance – how to walk and stand, and how the two bodies related to each other – both by doing exercises and by dancing with someone who was already skilled in the dance. As social conventions meant that a woman would follow rather than lead in public, her training did not need to go any further, but those who were interested would go on to lead – though always in private.

Because there were no formal 'classes' of the kind we have now come to expect in the modern Tango scene, people sometimes make the mistake of thinking that the men who danced in Buenos Aires were self-taught, but that is to misunderstand completely the process of the práctica. Men who danced in the Golden Age always spoke with reverence and warmth about the men from whom they learned. In a society where formal education stopped at the age of eleven, apprenticeship was the normal way of acquiring any skill, and young men expected to learn by studying a master, rather than by being taught.

In the absence of classes, there was no need for the master to articulate or to rationalise the way that he danced in order to instruct the person who was learning, as someone teaching a class must, and no need for the beginner to understand intellectually what he was learning to do with his body. (This meant that when Tango classes first appeared in the 1980s, few of the people who knew most about Tango could explain what they were doing when they danced in a way that new dancers could comprehend, as they had never had it explained verbally to them when they themselves were beginners.) Instead, a newcomer to the práctica learned the way a child learns a language, first absorbing the language from the fluent speakers around it, then after about nine months starting to speak the occasional word, gradually gaining confidence and skill, until after about three years the child can have a reasonable conversation. Beginners would be a minority in the práctica, and they would be surrounded by people who danced well, so their mistakes would not be compounded, as they often are in a setting where beginners outnumber experts. They had many models of excellence to aspire to, and personal experience of what did and did not feel good to the follower. They were not working out how to do the dance for themselves. They were absorbing the accumulated wisdom of the many generations who had walked the path before them.

Strikers dancing on a beach in 1912

There was a hierarchy in the práctica. The younger men looked up to the best and most experienced dancers in their own práctica, and were guided by them. If an older dancer thought something that a younger one was doing was inelegant or not in good taste, then the younger dancer would be told never to do it again – and the younger man would comply (or would at least be careful not to repeat it in front of the men he looked up to in his práctica). That relationship continued over the years, even if the young man was becoming well known in the milongas as a good dancer – or even if he went on to become a professional dancer performing in shows in theatres (or, towards the end of the Golden Age, on television).

The práctica was not just a place where new dancers went to learn the dance. It was an important part of the lives of all male Tango dancers. Men continued to go to the práctica for a couple of hours each night before they went to a milonga, and would often go on to the milonga together as a group.

Even in the 1990s, I was lucky enough to be invited to join a small group of men who had gone to the same práctica in the 1940s and 1950s, and who still got together to practise, and to get comments on how to improve their dancing from people they respected. The first time they invited me to join them it was because one of them had seen me leading. Although there was some resistance to women leading in milongas in Buenos Aires (I was always careful only to lead in a place where it would be acceptable), I was surprised by how often a man who learned in the Golden Age would react to seeing me lead by wanting to help me become a better leader, just as they had been helped by the older leaders in their prácticas when they themselves were young.

Within the práctica, experienced men often had regular dance partners. There would sometimes be demonstrations in the práctica, and the standard was expected to be higher than it was for the professional couples (with a man leading and a woman following) who danced in theatres. The men worked extremely hard to become the best dancers they could be, and used the prácticas to stretch themselves, as a safe place to make their mistakes. When a man had the opportunity to dance socially with a woman he made her comfort and pleasure his first priority, so he would never put himself in a position where he might make a mistake, and make her uncomfortable.

Men and women did not go to classes together and learn a repertoire of steps. No man could assume that when he danced with a woman she would know what movement she 'should' do next. He had to be able to lead every part of every movement. Indeed, the men took great delight in creating choreographic patterns that the follower could not have danced before, as a way of proving to anyone who might be watching how well they led.

There was only one definition of what it meant to be a good male Tango dancer that mattered – the best dancer was the one that gave the woman the best experience.

THE MAN'S ROLE AND THE WOMAN'S ROLE

In the milonga men danced one role and women danced the other. The English-speaking Tango community generally uses the terms 'leader' and 'follower' to describe those roles, because they are not gender specific. These terms do not come to us from Tango, but from the Ballroom community, and they can be taken to imply a hierarchical relationship, with the 'leader' having higher status than the 'follower'. The vocabulary used by the dancers of the Golden Age implied no such value judgement.

Often when a man who had learned to dance in the prácticas asked me to lead him, he would say that he would dance the woman's role, and I would dance the man's. He would see no contradiction in that. The two roles were easily labelled the man's role and the woman's role, because that was how they were divided in the milongas of the Golden Age, but the expectation in the práctica was that all the men danced both roles (and that if they chose to, in the home, when they danced together, women also danced both roles). It would not occur to him to think that he could not dance the woman's role

The shortage of women in Buenos Aires ensured that that definition was the only important one. It did not matter how good a man looked when he danced, or how many steps he knew. If a man made a woman uncomfortable in any way, she, quite rightly, would not dance with him again, and nor would any other woman who had seen what he had done. In the práctica each man experienced what it was like to dance with someone who led well, and what it felt like when something went wrong. If a man wanted the best women to dance with him, he knew from personal experience that respect for the follower had to be the foundation of everything he did as a leader.

To a man who danced in the Golden Age, if the follower was not because he was a man. All men danced it. To him that would be obvious.

In describing what the leader does, dancers of the Golden Age often used the verb *llevar*, a verb which has a number of possible translations, including to carry, to take, or to wear – a very different idea from the one implied by the verb 'to lead'. (It does not mean, though, that the leader was literally carrying the weight of the follower's body through the dance.)

In describing what the follower does, a number of different verbs were used. One was to allow (*dejar*) oneself to be carried (*llevado*). Another was *acompañar* – to accompany.

But *acompañar* could also be used to describe what the leader was doing, especially when discussing turning steps. This represents a fundamental truth about the relationship between the leader and follower as understood by the dancers of the Golden Age. To lead was in fact to follow the follower. This paradox lies at the heart of the choreographic freedom enjoyed by Tango dancers in the Golden Age. It is by following the follower that the leader gets the power to carry the follower wherever the leader wishes.

treated with respect and dignity, then whatever the steps might be and whatever the music might be, the dance was not Tango.

That is not to say that the men got no pleasure from leading – far from it! The relationship between the leader and follower that gives the maximum pleasure to the follower, once it has been understood, also gives maximum pleasure to the leader.

This is the essence of what makes Tango unique. Because of its environment, it evolved as a dance whose aim was the giving of pleasure to the other person, with the understanding that giving pleasure to the other person was the wisest road to pleasure for oneself.

MACHISMO AND THE TANGO

Tango is often perceived as a macho dance. The man leads, and the woman follows. The man gives the orders and the woman does as she is told. Natural as this assumption may seem, it is to misunderstand the nature of the dance as it was done in Buenos Aires in the Golden Age. In order to learn 'the man's role', a man was expected to put himself into 'the woman's role' until he completely understood it – until he had felt from personal experience exactly what the woman wanted and needed for her comfort and pleasure. Only once he had completely understood what the woman went through in dancing the Tango was he allowed to start learning 'the man's role'. This is, in fact, the antithesis of machismo.

A dear friend of mine who learned to dance in the 1940s once said to me, 'I don't want a woman to say, "You are a wonderful dancer," I want her to say, "How sweet it is to dance with you."' (*Que dulce que es bailar con tigo.*)

Even the way in which a man and a woman came together to dance in the milongas was far less macho than it seemed. The man always walked over to the woman and led her onto the dance floor, and at the end of the dance he returned her to her place. But the agreement to dance was made by the *cabezeo* – by making eye contact, and then a small gesture of the head. This was not something the man could initiate if the woman was not willing. And the woman could catch the man's eye as easily as he

Men Dancing with Women

A friend of mine who had learned to dance in the early 1950s described to me his first experience of dancing with a woman. He had been going to a práctica regularly for three years, and took his dancing extremely seriously. One day he found himself at a wedding. An older man from his práctica was there with his girlfriend, and could catch hers. A man would not approach a woman who had not made eye contact with him. She had as much power in the choice of partners as he did.

And the man returned the woman to her place at the end of the dance not because he was in charge, but because if the follower had been completely involved in the dance, she might be disorientated, and might appreciate the courtesy of being guided back to her seat.

While it cannot be denied that Argentina in the first half of the twentieth century was a very macho place in most respects, machismo was not inherent in the nature of Tango.

Curiously, while our own society today is much more equal in general, in the Tango the modern idea that a man will only learn to lead (without learning to follow), and a woman will only learn to follow, has brought a new kind of machismo to the dance floor that did not exist in the Golden Age. In a milonga a man walks up to a woman and asks her to dance, putting social pressure on her to dance with him whether she wants to or not, and disempowering her, forcing her either to become passive and wait to be asked, or aggressive in pursuing the partner of her choice. And the dance itself changes when a leader without the skill of following is not able to follow the follower in the way the leaders of the Golden Age did – which in turn may force the follower to follow in a different way. Without the understanding of the follower's role that leaders once had, it becomes possible for leaders to dance with a machismo that the leaders of the Golden Age would have found unacceptable.

suggested to my friend that he and the woman have a dance. 'I took the woman in my arms,' my friend said, 'and I forgot everything.'

For the majority of men in the Golden Age the main reason to go to a milonga was to dance with women. Another reason was to dance to live music – all the great Tango bands of the period played live for dancers – but for most men the presence of women was the main attraction.

Dancing in the street in Buenos Aires

What a Man Wanted from a Woman in the Milonga

In Ballet the ideal woman is an ethereal creature, almost lighter than air. In some couple dances the ideal follower is one who is so light that the leader almost does not know that the follower is there.

In the Golden Age of Tango a man went to a milonga because he wanted to hold a flesh-and-blood woman in his arms. He wanted to meet and connect with an individual. He did not want a follower who was so light that he did not know she was there. That is not to say that he wanted a follower to be heavy or to be hard to move. What he wanted to feel was presence.

It is easy to assume that the more important person in a couple is the leader. But the social environment in Buenos Aires during the creation of Tango meant that the more important person was the follower. Women were precious and rare creatures, heavily outnumbered by the men in any milonga. Women who were good dancers were even rarer.

So a woman who could dance well had a high status in the milonga, and her awareness of her status was part of what made her a good dancer, as it gave her the confidence to wait.

It is common for inexperienced or insecure followers to assume they will dance better by trying to 'do the right thing', that is, by trying to guess what step the leader wants the follower to do, and then doing it without putting the leader to the inconvenience of leading it. The follower may be afraid of not feeling or understanding the lead, or may simply be trying to be helpful. If the leader's aim is to create a beautiful choreography that looks wonderful to anyone watching the couple from the outside, or if the leader's main interest is in taking pleasure in his or her own dancing, then a follower who 'does the right thing' all the time may be the ideal – and dancing pre-choreographed routines may be even more effective.

But if the leader's aim is to connect with the real individual standing in front of him or her, then dancing with a follower who constantly tries to 'do the right thing' – even if that follower does indeed do the step the leader wanted most of the time – feels as frustrating as trying to catch hold of smoke.

What a man in the Golden Age of Tango was searching for was a woman who waited – a woman whose presence he could feel, and who did not move unless he moved her.

Waiting takes confidence, and trust in the leader's ability to lead. The follower was not being passive, but was allowing the leader to take care of her or him, and waiting to be given the pleasure of the dance.

Dealing with Reality

While dancing, the leader is steering the journey of the couple, and with each movement will have an expectation that a certain result will be produced in the position of the follower's feet.

Sometimes that just does not happen.

This is reality. To the men who learned to dance in the Golden Age, it was the leader's responsibility to deal with it, whatever the reason for the unexpected outcome – whether it was the leader's fault, the follower's fault, or just one of those things.

It was not the follower's responsibility to put right anything that had gone wrong, even if it had been the follower's fault. Indeed, the leaders of the Golden Age never allowed the follower to feel that she

However, in one-to-one combat a person must be completely focused on where the other person is at all times, and must constantly adapt his or her own movement to that reality. Allowing the focus to slip from the other person for an instant could result in defeat, and possibly a great deal of pain. The martial arts share with Tango the need to be completely aware of where another person is at all times.

Tango and the martial arts are also both based on natural movement, rather than the aesthetically pleasing modifications of natural movement that are at the heart of performance dance.

So while people with experience of the martial arts, but no dance training, may at first struggle with moving to the music, or with learning figures, they nevertheless come to Tango with some important skills already in place, and tend to progress quickly.

or he had made a mistake. They instantly repaired the relationship between the two bodies and reinvented the plan, with every step if necessary. As one older dancer once said to me, 'If the woman goes wrong, I go wrong with her', by which he meant, if the follower goes somewhere that was not where I intended, I follow the follower to where she or he actually is. They knew that this was the only way to regain control. They could only change reality by first accepting it.

Indeed, some men took particular pleasure in finding solutions to the choreographic challenge posed by occasionally finding the couple in an unexpected position.

A follower is not a robot. The men in the milongas knew they were dancing with a flesh-and-blood woman, and they were very glad of it, even if she might make the occasional mistake. Not all followers danced equally well. A beginner with poor technique, or who tried to 'do the right thing' and guess what step was coming next rather than waiting, would inevitably end up in the wrong place from time to time. But the reality was that the leader was dancing with *this* follower, poor technique or excellent technique, constant guesswork or meditative stillness.

The follower is where the follower is. To the leaders of the Golden Age, that was their only reality. If the follower was not where the plan in the leader's head would have taken her or him, then it was not the follower who was wrong, but the plan in the leader's head, which had become useless and should be immediately discarded. To carry on with the plan regardless of where the follower actually was ('I led it correctly, so *I'm* not wrong!') would have seemed to them to be the height of stupidity. The experience of the dance for both leader and follower would have been ruined.

The leader wanted a follower who waited. The follower could only wait if she or he could trust the leader at all times, throughout the dance. The leader could only be trusted if he or she was prepared to deal with reality.

The Physical and Emotional Relationship Between the Leader and the Follower

In the competitive Ballroom dances, the leader and follower stand slightly to one side of each other, with their bodies making a V shape. The leader's upper right arm becomes an extension of the leader's shoulders, and the follower is placed in the space made by the leader's bent right arm.

Ballroom position

This position has many practical advantages. From the point of view of someone who is a complete beginner trying to dance with another complete beginner in a class, it places the leader's and follower's feet on different parallel lines, so it reduces the danger of treading on each other's toes – a major worry for beginners in any dance. In fact beginners tend to adopt this position naturally for that reason. Once they have become used to it, it can be hard to dance in any other way, so dances that are passed on through beginners' classes tend over time to adapt to suit this position.

It is not, though, the most natural and intimate way for two people who care about each other to embrace.

In a natural, loving hug, two people generally stand directly in front of each other, with their shoulders parallel, and the centres of their bodies aligned. They are standing heart to heart.

Tango position

Two people in this position are saying to each other with their body language that they are giving each other their complete and undivided attention. They are each placing the other member of the couple at the centre of their universe, making that person the most important thing in their world. The direction in which the heart is pointed reveals what matters to us much more clearly than the direction in which we are looking.

Tango evolved in a society where loneliness and isolation were the norm, where many people were forced to live on their own, and where attention and true intimacy were rare and precious. Naturally, then, Tango dancers chose the most intimate, personal, and perhaps even emotionally challenging position possible in which to dance. Tango dancers of the Golden Age danced with the shoulders parallel, and the centres of the bodies aligned.

They danced heart to heart.

THE HEART

In discussing the relationship between the leader and the follower I am going to refer frequently to the two hearts. This is not quite anatomically correct. The physical heart is placed slightly to the left of the centre of the body. I am speaking metaphorically, about the emotional centre – a place at the level of the heart, but precisely at the centre of the body. Some people might refer to it as the heart chakra or heart centre – the part of the body that resonates with loving energy.

Even though this is not exactly where the physical heart is placed, the word conveys the meaning, so I shall use it when I mean the centre of the upper body.

Movement Puts the Unity of the Two Hearts to the Test

In life it is change that helps us discover who our true friends are. In Tango it is movement that proves whether we are truly together, or merely in front of each other. Only if my partner's heart continues to be pointed directly at mine, whatever happens, whatever the dance may bring to us, do I know that my partner is committed to me. If my partner's heart slips away from me, then I know my partner's attention has wandered. I am not the most important thing in my partner's world at that moment.

To the dancers of the Golden Age, nothing mattered more than the person in their arms. Their focus never wavered for an instant. Whether they were great dancers or undistinguished ones, whichever style of Tango they danced, this part of the experience of dancing with them was always the same.

The room moved around us. The floor beneath us shifted. Our legs, whose function was to help our hearts stay together and motionless, folded and stepped, allowing our two hearts to remain completely still, completely united, as the world changed around us. Unity and stillness in the face of motion proved that for three minutes we were not two dancers, but one couple.

To the dancers of the Golden Age, this was the purpose of Tango.

How the Dancers of the Golden Age Avoided Treading on Each Other's Toes

While dancing in this position gives the couple the greatest emotional connection, it poses a serious practical problem. How do you move without treading on your partner's toes? How does the leader take a step forwards, knowing that the follower is directly in front? Obviously, treading on a woman's toes in a milonga would have been unacceptable. It was necessary for the men to find a way of moving that put the follower at no risk of pain, or even discomfort.

When I asked the men who learned to dance in the prácticas how to walk forwards in the Tango, they always said that one should walk naturally, in the same way that one walks down the street. And it is true that those men did walk down the street in the same way that they walked on the dance floor. It is also true that they spent countless hours working on how to walk forwards in the dance. What seemed a natural way of walking to them is not natural to most other people (including most modern citizens of Buenos Aires) — or at least not without a fair amount of practice.

For those men, a step forwards did not begin with a movement of the foot, or a movement of the knee, as it tends to for most people. It began with a movement of the heart. The free foot, passively hanging from the body, moved with the heart, taking the body's weight only when necessary to prevent the body from falling. Many years ago when I was studying mime, I was taught a walk called 'The Walk of the Matador' that was very similar. This confident, elegant way of moving would be impossible with the shoulders slumped forwards, or with any stiffness or tension in the legs.

A step back for the follower and forwards for the leader

1) Initiation

The movement begins, as do all movements in Tango, in the leader's heart. The leader moves his or her body directly towards the follower's heart.

2) Extension

The follower's body moves with the leader's body (as it does at all times). Before the movement is large enough for the follower to be consciously aware of it, the follower's free foot extends back, with the toes flat on the floor, but with no weight on them.

By moving forwards with the heart first, before moving the leg, the leader could lead the follower to move back so that the follower's toes were no longer there when the leader's foot arrived, and there was no danger of their being trodden on. The leader moved directly towards and then through the follower's heart, carrying the follower's heart back. The follower in turn waited to be carried. The follower did not move the heart, but allowed the leader to carry it back. That way the two hearts stayed together and motionless, even as the step took place, and the emotional connection within the couple remained constant.

Taking a Single Step

In Buenos Aires in the Golden Age a beginner never had to try to dance with another beginner. A person who was new to the Tango, whether that person was a woman or a man, only danced with experienced

3) Transfer

As the leader's body continues to move straight towards the follower's body, the leader carries the follower's body back, transferring the follower's weight from the front foot to the back foot. The follower's front leg travels with the follower's body, so by the time the follower's body is over the back foot, the follower's front foot is by its side. The leader's front foot arrives directly under the leader's body, which is directly in front of the follower's body, at the same moment, taking the leader's weight.

4) Conclusion

The leader allows the back leg to fall into place next to the leg bearing the leader's weight.

For Key to the Illustrations see p7.

dancers. Only once they were themselves experienced would they ever find themselves dancing with a beginner, and almost without exception that would be an experienced leader dancing with an inexperienced follower. Before a person started to lead, they would already understand the way that Tango worked, and, most importantly, they would already have learned how to walk.

When I first started to try to walk backwards the way skilled Tango dancers did, I found it immensely frustrating. I came to Tango with a dance background, and I'd always found that I could go into any dance class and pick up the steps with no real trouble – once you've learned the skill of picking up steps, learning new steps is pretty straightforward, so I could take in fairly complicated routines without too much difficulty.

But I couldn't walk backwards correctly, and my years of Ballet and Ballroom as a child didn't help – except, I suppose, that they helped me to be aware of where my body was and realise it wasn't doing what I wanted it to do. And if I couldn't walk backwards correctly then I wasn't really able to allow myself to be led. A highly skilled Tango leader could give me the illusion that I was following perfectly – that is an important part of the leader's skill in Tango! – but the reality was that until I learned to walk backwards correctly I would never give that leader a dance that allowed them to experience the higher levels of Tango.

Fortunately, while walking backwards correctly is not easy, learning the skill is only a matter of patience and application. It does not take special talents. Anyone who can walk can learn to do it, provided they understand what they are trying to achieve, and put in some regular practice. And once walking backwards correctly has been mastered, learning to walk forwards correctly becomes relatively straightforward.

The men who learned to dance in the prácticas rarely analysed exactly how they did what they did, beyond understanding the exercises they needed to master in order to dance well. Though few would have been consciously aware of it, a step back for the follower and forwards for the leader was made up of several different parts (See box on P.34).

The thing that frustrated me when I first tried to walk backwards in this way was that I could not extend my foot back without moving my body back, and putting weight on my back foot. But if I moved my own body back at the same time as I moved my foot, I would be pulling my heart away from my partner, giving a skilled leader the sensation that I was running away from him or her, and tearing apart the connection between our two hearts (even though I myself might not be aware that anything was wrong). Learning to allow my leader to move my heart, and not to move it myself, was a real challenge to me – as it is to many people who come to Tango with some dance training, since we are used to being in complete control of our own movements. But I practised my exercises every day, and in only a few weeks the difference was great enough for all the leaders I danced with to comment on it.

This way of walking takes time and effort to learn. Two complete beginners standing together in their first class have almost no chance of being able to do it correctly. However, this way of walking allows the couple to keep the two hearts united at all times while dancing, giving the most connected and emotionally satisfying dance possible.

But it does more than that. Where most social dances rely on both dancers knowing some routines, even if those routines may sometimes be made up of only two or three steps, Tango allows much greater choreographic freedom. The leader is able to lead not just each individual step that the follower takes, but each part of each step, which means that the couple can, if the leader chooses, create extraordinarily complex patterns on the dance floor. The same technique that gives the most emotionally satisfying dance also gives the most choreographically liberated dance.

This is the secret of the blend of sex and chess that makes Tango so uniquely intoxicating.

The Attitude of the Men to their Own Feet

I was once watching a man who had learned to dance in a práctica showing a group of young dancers a figure – a series of movements. He took one of the women and led her through it. One of the men asked him to demonstrate the figure again, so he took the woman and led her through it once more. The young man protested that the second time it had been a different figure. The older man disagreed. It had been the same figure. The young man would not be convinced. It had been a different figure, he insisted – the older man had done something completely different with his feet. 'Oh yes,' the older man replied. 'I was on the other foot. But it was the same figure.'

On another occasion a young man I knew asked an older dancer to show him some turning steps. The older dancer took his partner and led her through a beautiful turning combination. 'That was wonderful,' my friend said. 'What did you do?'

'We went that way,' the older man replied, indicating the direction of the turn of the hearts with his hand.

'But what did you do?'

'We went that way,' the older man said again, starting to get puzzled.

'But what did you do with your feet?' my friend asked.

'With my feet? Oh, um, well, I suppose I did something like this . . .'

These stories illustrate a fundamental truth about what the men who learned in the prácticas thought of as important in the Tango. What mattered was the follower's movement. No matter how complicated the things they chose to do with their own feet, the purpose of the leader's movement was to facilitate the follower's movement. Which foot the leader happened to be on was insignificant. It was the movement the follower was making that mattered.

Tango took place not on the level of the floor, but on the level of the hearts. The movement of the feet was a symptom of the movement of the hearts, caused by it, not causing it. It was the follower's heart that danced. The leader's job was to make that happen.

The leader's heart was the most important part of the leader's body because it was used to move the follower's heart. The follower's feet mattered, because the leader would never try to make the follower do something that was physically impossible – the follower cannot move one leg through the other as they are both solid, nor can the follower move the foot the follower is standing on. The leader needed to know where the follower's feet were in order to know what movements the follower's body could make. This was the leader's responsibility, not the follower's. With a competent leader the follower would not need to pay any attention to the movement of her or his own feet.

The leader's feet served only one function in the dance – they were there to stop the leader's heart from falling on the floor. Anything more than that was pure decoration.

THE LEADER'S AND FOLLOWER'S FEET MAY DO
DIFFERENT THINGS

The salida of northern Buenos Aires is an example of a step where the leader took only two steps, while leading the follower to take four. It illustrates the way in which the two dancers can do quite different things with their feet.

The easiest way to visualise this step is to imagine how a first dance there might begin. During the Golden Age, in a milonga the single women would be seated at tables, while the single men often preferred to stand at the bar. A man standing at the bar would be scanning the room, looking for a woman he wanted to dance with, and trying to make eye contact with her. The women seated at tables would be scanning the room trying to make eye contact with a suitable man. Once they had established eye contact, and, with a gesture of the head, one had invited the other to dance, and the other, with a smile and a nod, had agreed, it would be the man who would walk up to the woman's table (whether he had asked her to dance or she had asked him), and only when he arrived in front of her would she stand up. They would then take the embrace of the dance.

At this moment, they were at the edge of the dance floor, and as he took her right hand in his left, the joined hands were pointing in the direction of the line of flow of dancers around the floor.

How should they take their first step? In a milonga in Buenos Aires in the Golden Age, a leader would never begin the dance by taking a step back, any more than a driver would suddenly reverse from traffic lights. The leader couldn't see what was going on behind him, and suddenly taking a step backwards into the dancing couples would be dangerous, as it could easily lead to a collision.

The leader would also not start the dance with a step forwards. Although he would be able to see what was happening in front of him, they were at the edge of the dance floor, so there would be nowhere for them to go.

A step to the side was considered the ideal way to start a dance, and as they were standing with the joined hands pointing in the direction of the line of dance, naturally the ideal step to take would be a side step in that direction, that is, along the line of the joined hands, which would be with the right for the follower.

This posed the problem of what step they should take next. Straight forwards for the leader was still out of the question, as they would be carried off the dance floor. A side step in the opposite direction would take them against the flow of movement around the dance floor, and back to where they started. A step back would still be a dangerous option because of oncoming traffic. So the solution was for the leader to turn the follower, leading the follower to step back with the left, more or less in the direction of the line of dance.

In the northern areas of Buenos Aires, this is the way in which the leader would lead these two steps for the follower:

The leader leads the follower's extension, then turns the follower's heart anticlockwise to lead the transfer of the follower's weight. This allows the leader to complete the follower's first step while his or her own weight is kept back.

The leader then leads the follower's second step by moving straight towards the follower's heart.

So the leader had succeeded in leading the follower to take two steps, while the leader had taken just one.

The leader would then lead the follower to take two more steps, again while taking only one step, to finish the pattern.

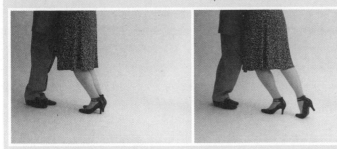

The leader leads the follower's extension.

While leading the transfer the leader turns the follower's heart anticlockwise again, carrying it, and the follower's left leg which hangs from it, across the follower's right leg, so that the follower's weight goes onto the left, with the legs crossed.

The couple is now moving in the direction of the flow around the dance floor.

Of course, once a leader had enough skill to have complete control of the follower's movement, the leader was free to do with his or her own feet whatever pleased the leader's taste and musicality. The leader could take two or more steps while the follower took one, or could lead the follower to take several steps while barely moving his or her own feet at all. Men in the prácticas competed to find better and more interesting combinations that they could add to their repertoire. Being able to maintain the correct relationship with their follower at all times and yet also do complex things with their own feet showed that leaders were highly skilled. But concentrating on doing complex things with the feet and losing the relationship with the follower would have seemed to them absurd and self-defeating. To them it would have been completely to misunderstand the meaning of Tango.

The Skill of the Follower

The social reality of Buenos Aires during the Golden Age meant that women did not go to classes to learn the Tango. We tend to assume that learning a dance means learning a repertoire of steps. The follower did not do that, nor did becoming a better follower involve learning a larger repertoire, as it does in some other dances. Instead the follower trained her or his body to move correctly with the leader's body. Becoming a better follower involved being more accurate, more finely balanced and having greater stillness.

The leader led the follower's extension back or to the side by moving the follower's heart sufficiently to take the follower's body imperceptibly off its axis. A novice follower sometimes needs to be taken quite a long way out of balance before she or he takes a step. As the follower improves, the movement of the heart needed to lead the extension of the foot becomes smaller and smaller. In the práctica the men learned to lead and follow with precision, and the more precise the leader is, the easier it is for the follower's body to become trained to be finely balanced.

If the follower always waited for the leader to lead not just each step, but each part of each step, then at any time the leader could lead the follower to do anything.

The perfect follower needed to be able to stand perfectly, extend the free foot back or to the side perfectly, allow the leader to transfer the follower's weight perfectly, maintain the relationship between the two hearts perfectly, turn perfectly and wait perfectly. (Perfectly, of course, means in the perfect way for Tango. Other dances have different ways of moving and of relating to the partner, so someone with perfect technique in another dance will find they cannot do these things in the perfect Tango way without training, and vice versa.) If the follower could do all those things then the follower could follow anything any leader dancing any style of Tango led, from the simplest combination to the most complicated, including the spectacular kicks and flicks so loved by Tango performers.

A leader was able to choose not to lead movements that the leader was not technically competent to perform, or that did not suit the leader's body. The follower did not have that luxury. A great follower had to be able to do whatever the leader chose to lead.

So while it is undoubtedly easier for a complete beginner to learn to follow a little than to learn to lead a little, and while a novice follower finds it easy to have a wonderful time following a highly skilled leader (because it is an important part of the leader's skill to give the follower that feeling) at the next level, following is harder than leading.

An accomplished follower rose beyond the technical skills of standing, walking and waiting. In order to allow her or his body to be taken in whichever direction the leader chose, the follower needed to abandon the left-brain activity that normally keeps us safe through our daily lives, and shut down the mechanisms of self-preservation that prevent us from getting run over as we cross the street. The follower had to stop taking any responsibility for her or his own safety, so as to be able to stop taking any responsibility for her or his movement through the room – the follower needed to give up that responsibility to the leader. In this way the follower allowed the leader to lead. In order to truly follow, the follower entered a kind of active meditative state.

THE SUBTLETY AND PRECISION OF THE LEAD

One of the characteristic movements for the follower in the Tango of the Golden Age is the cross (*cruce*), where the leader leads the follower to extend the right foot back, but then, instead of finishing the step back as normal, the leader turns the follower's heart during the transfer, carrying it, and therefore the follower's left foot (which hangs passively from the follower's heart), across and in front of the follower's right foot.

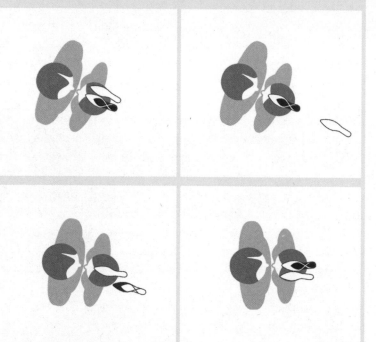

This movement can only be done correctly if the two hearts are completely united, if the leader is completely aware of the follower's movement, and if the follower steps back correctly. The difference for the follower between being led into the cross and being led into a normal step back is tremendously subtle – too subtle for the follower to be able to work out intellectually which movement the leader intended, and 'do' the step. The follower can only wait, and allow the leader to carry the follower's heart to the correct place.

Starting position

Final position – step back

Starting position

Final position – cross

The difference for the follower between the two final positions is a turn that carries the follower's heart little more than the width of the follower's foot

This makes it an extremely difficult movement for two beginners to do correctly in their first Tango class. However, the movement is so ubiquitous in Tango choreography that it is often one of the first things that beginners learn, and sometimes, as a kind of shorthand, they are taught it as though it is part of a routine, and that at certain moments the follower is expected to cross, and should do so without waiting to be led.

This would never have happened in Buenos Aires in the Golden Age.

Dancing movements this subtle flawlessly requires the dancers' skills to be developed to a certain level – a level that was the norm in the Golden Age.

This was an unusual kind of meditative state, in that it was externalised rather than internalised. The follower was focused completely on the leader, the other member of the couple, and was not withdrawing into a private, inner world. It was a generous act – the abandonment of the self into the other.

In order to allow that to happen the follower had to be able to trust the leader completely, and the leader needed constantly to deserve that trust.

The Responsibility of the Leader

Once a follower had given up her or his normal mechanisms of self-preservation, if the leader made a movement that did not respect the follower's axis, therefore compromising the follower's balance, the follower was in danger of discomfort or even, at extremes, injury. The more finely tuned the follower's balance – that is to say, the more skilled the follower was – the more potential danger the follower would be in if the leader did not treat the follower with care and respect. Putting the follower at risk of discomfort or injury was considered unacceptable.

Collisions on the dance floor were also unacceptable, as the follower had to be protected. While it is impossible to avoid all collisions on a crowded dance floor, it was astonishing to see how rarely the leaders who learned in the prácticas collided with other couples, even on impossibly packed floors, and even when doing what seemed to be very complicated figures. Fitting the dance to the space available and avoiding collisions was considered an important part of the leader's skill.

The leader's first priority at all times was to keep the follower safe. The leader had to be focused on respecting the follower's balance, and had to care for the follower's safety as devotedly as someone would care for the safety of a small child who has not yet learned to understand danger. The follower had placed her or his own safety in the leader's hands. The leader needed to take responsibility for it completely and consistently.

At any moment if the leader compromised the follower's comfort the follower's self-preservation mechanisms might kick in. It takes a great deal of presence of mind and determination for a follower to prevent that from happening. Whether the follower managed to continue to follow or not, the follower would certainly be jolted out of the meditative state that accompanies following at the higher levels – if the follower had managed to reach that state at all during the dance – and reaching the state again in that dance would become much harder.

When the follower is concerned for her or his own safety, rather than being able to trust it to the leader, there is a great deal of pressure on the follower to anticipate. To people who learned to dance during the Golden Age, that was not Tango.

For this reason, the care of the follower's comfort and safety was at all times the priority of leaders who learned to dance in the práctica. Part of that is, of course, simple good manners – if you want someone to dance with you then it is only right that you should make them feel as comfortable as possible. However, the main reason was much less altruistic. The more perfectly the follower followed, the better a dance the leader would get, the greater flexibility the leader would have to create choreographic shapes in the free-flowing improvisation of the dance floor, the more control the leader would have, and the more connection the leader would feel. The follower could only give the leader what the leader wanted if the leader could be completely trusted, and the leader could only be completely trusted if the leader made the follower's safety the first priority in the dance. In order to get complete control of the follower's movements, the leader needed to make the follower the centre of his or her world.

If the leader's focus slipped for an instant from the follower, then the follower's trust would be lost, and the leader would have to work to regain it. If for an instant the leader's heart was not directly in front of the follower's heart, the follower would feel it, and the follower's ability to follow would be compromised.

So, paradoxically, it was by giving his or her whole focus to the follower that the leader was able to create the richest and most satisfying experience for him or herself.

The principle that one receives most pleasure by abandoning thoughts of one's own pleasure, and concentrating on giving pleasure to one's partner instead, is one that is familiar to students of Yogic and Taoist theories of relationships. With no apparent knowledge of these ancient spiritual traditions, Tango dancers discovered in the prácticas and milongas of Buenos Aires that the best dance came not from focusing on one's own dancing pleasure, but from abandoning oneself into one's partner.

THE RELATIONSHIP WITH THE MUSIC

Most dances are defined by a rhythm. The music created for the dance sets up that rhythm for the dancers, and the steps are designed to fit into the rhythm in a specific way. If the dancers place the steps into the rhythm any other way, they are said to be 'off the music'. That is not the case in Tango. There is no rhythm section in an orquesta típica – the Argentinian Tango band. Instead, the interweaving melodic lines of the different instruments offer the dancers a variety of possibilities at any moment. Each piece of music has a rhythmic structure subtly different from the next. Experienced dancers allow themselves to be inspired by the music, moulding their movements into their own unique interpretation of it.

The music becomes the third member of the couple, drawing out of the couple choreographic shapes they would otherwise never have created, and deepening the communication between the dancers.

Improvisation and the 'Vulcan Mind Meld' – The Ultimate Level of Tango

Tango as danced in the Golden Age was structured in a way that was similar to a language. Steps or figures – the little choreographed routines that define our understanding of many other dances – were like poems or quotations that the leader may have learned from someone else, or may have invented in a práctica. There can be great pleasure in throwing a quotation into one's conversation, and learning poems can be a good way of becoming more articulate. Still, while it might be possible to choose to speak only in quotations from Shakespeare, it would be a strange way to live a life. To the dancers of the Golden Age, only dancing figures would have been a strange way to dance the Tango.

Dancers of that generation often talked about 'walking' (caminando) the Tango. When I first heard this term, I assumed it meant keeping it simple, and avoiding showy movements, but I quickly learned that it meant nothing of the sort. Often the people who spoke most about walking their Tango were the people who did the most complex and eye-catching things on the dance floor. What they meant was not that the dance should be simple, but that it should be free. They would lead the follower to take a step in one direction, and then another step, perhaps in a different direction. Each step that they led the follower to take had its own existence and life in that moment. Nothing happened because it was the next step in the sequence. Each individual step was a response to the moment, the music and the space available on the dance floor. When they talked about walking the Tango, what they meant was that it should be danced with the ease with which one walks down the street, moving one foot and then the other, with no forethought, existing completely in the moment. What they meant was what we would call improvisation.

But when they used the word improvisando, they meant something else. When dancers who danced in the Golden Age talked about improvisation, they were referring to a higher level – the ultimate level of Tango to which they all aspired. This was the level where not only the follower but also the leader accessed the active meditative state, abandoning the self into the other, when a new creature was created with one heart leading all four feet, and being led by the music.

At this level both the emotional experience of the dance and the choreographic expression of it are at their most profound. To see a couple dancing at this level is unforgettable – to experience it is even more so.

The first time I experienced it, I struggled to find a way to explain to my friends what had just happened. I could only find one, about as far removed from the Tango as it was possible to get. Bizarre as it was, the only image I could think of that explained it was one from *Star Trek*.

In the original *Star Trek* series one of the characters had the ability to put his hands onto another being and fuse their two minds, so that they shared their memories and thoughts, and became, for a moment, one being. He called it the 'Vulcan Mind Meld'. This was the only image I could find that came close to explaining the sense of being completely known, completely understood and completely accepted that I had just experienced.

To reach this level both the leader and the follower must be in the active meditative state in which the self is abandoned into the other. It is impossible for the leader to reach this meditative state if the follower has not reached it. If the follower stops following the leader even to the smallest degree, then the leader must be jolted back to an everyday consciousness. And it is impossible for the follower to reach the meditative state if the leader breaks the follower's trust even for an instant.

So good technique, as the dancers of the Golden Age defined it, in keeping the hearts united at all times and focusing both dancers on each other, not on themselves, became a mechanism designed to make the highest level of Tango easier to access.

Of course, this is not the only way to enjoy a dance. There is much delight to be gained from playfully and spontaneously creating a choreographic shape together that suits the music. As a leader I take great pleasure from making my follower laugh, which happens when we do a movement that fits, just so, into the music, perhaps with a shape traced on the floor that she or he was not expecting, or an interesting change of direction.

But to those who have experienced *improvisando* – improvising as the dancers of the Golden Age understood the word – it remains the holy grail of Tango experience, once glimpsed, always sought. It may happen out of the blue, even to those without much skill or experience of the Tango, when everything comes together in exactly the right way. When that happens without explanation, the dancers are inclined to believe that it is something mystical or unique. They return to the Tango again and again in search of it, without knowing what to do to increase the chances of repeating the experience in the future.

The dancers of the Golden Age understood that, while this state might occur spontaneously, the purpose of good technique was to make accessing it easier. Indeed the purpose of good technique in the Tango is to re-create what happens in those spontaneous moments – the coming together of two hearts into one.

Why Your Best Dance of the Evening May Actually Be With a Beginner

Golden Age Tango technique was designed to make it easier to bring the two hearts together, and in doing so to give the greatest sense of intimacy and connection with the other person while dancing. Training the body to move in the correct way allows each dancer to improve his or her own ability to connect with a partner.

Some people may come to the Tango already skilled in focusing their attention on another person and giving them their trust and respect, while other people may struggle with trust, or get caught up in their sense of their own dancing, not realising that they are not engaging with their partner as fully as they might, or that they are being disrespectful. Some people may come to Tango with a history of issues connected with their desire to dance, or with their relationships with other people, while others may be happily unencumbered by a sense of having anything to prove.

When someone comes to Tango with respect for their partner, with the willingness and ability to focus on the other person and to connect with them rather than concentrating on their own dancing, that person is already in tune with the meaning and purpose of Tango. Technical shortcomings may limit the actual steps that make up their first dance. But the experience of dancing with a complete beginner who has this attitude is far superior to the experience of dancing with someone who has spent months or years learning steps, but who does not engage with the partner.

For a person who comes to the Tango with the correct attitude and manages to maintain it, learning the skills of the dance will only make them more of a pleasure to dance with – the goal of any Golden Age dancer.

Some people get caught up in the process of learning steps, or find themselves distracted by other personal goals. Some choose to dance with a technique that is different from the technique used by the dancers of the Golden Age, and may then find they have selected a technique that makes it harder rather than easier for them to connect with their partner. (This may happen if the dancer's focus is on the stage rather than on social dance, or for many other reasons.) Some people may have had so many disappointing experiences of dancing with people who did not engage with them that they have lost the ability to trust their partner. So the length of time a person has been dancing may give little indication of how pleasant they will be to dance with – unless their experience of learning the dance has allowed them to learn at least part of what was learned by the people who danced in the prácticas and milongas of the Golden Age.

It is attitude that makes the Tango dancer. Skill improves the dancer, but attitude is the essence of skill. People who learned in Buenos Aires in the Golden Age learned the attitude as inseparable from the dance.

PART II

The History of Tango Music, Poetry and Dance
in Buenos Aires, and in the Rest of the World–

THE MANY FACES OF TANGO

A History of the Different Forms of Tango in Buenos Aires

To people outside the Spanish-speaking world, Tango is a dance. There is Tango music, of course, because a dance has to have music, so Tango music must be the music that goes with the dance. But Tango means dance.

That is not how Tango is seen in Argentina.

Many of the most passionate Tango enthusiasts in Argentina do not dance, do not know how to dance, and are not interested in the dance. Tango historians in Argentina rarely, if ever, study the history of the dance.

That may seem a terrible paradox. What is Tango if it is not a dance? The fact is, though, that in Argentina the dance is only a part of Tango, and dance music is only a part of Tango music.

Tango music is a wide and varied genre. To ask what Tango sounds like is like asking what Jazz sounds like — there are so many different answers to that question that it becomes meaningless. Like Jazz, Tango has its enthusiastic collectors, hunting down every obscure recording and knowing every fact about the great musicians. It has dance music and music that is designed for the concert platform, it has singers that take centre stage and others that perform as another instrument in the band, it has music arranged for big bands in big venues and music jammed by small groups in small, intimate spaces.

Tango dance and Tango music began together – or if they did not, they had become intertwined long before either had become anything we would recognise as Tango today. Very little reliable historical evidence exists about Tango in the nineteenth century, and inevitably the few facts available can be used to fit a number of different theories. There is one frequently repeated myth about the origin of Tango, though, that certainly is not true.

One of the most persistent clichés about the origin of Tango is that it was born in the brothels of Buenos Aires – an idea that has clearly captured many people's imagination.

The first written records of the dance tend to tie it to the brothels – the writer Jorge Luis Borges is frequently quoted as saying that he had been told that Tango had been born there. However, this says more about the nature of Argentinian society at that time than it does about Tango. The intellectual elite did not mix with the working class and immigrant community. The areas where the poor lived in the nineteenth century were like foreign countries to the rich, in much the same way that the East End, with its docks, its poverty and its immigrant communities, was an exotic and alien place to London's elite at that time.

Men of letters did not meet working-class people socially – or at least, not unless they went to a brothel.

Brothels were a major place of entertainment for the working classes, as well as being a significant employer of working-class women. By the 1890s the majority of the population of the city of Buenos Aires were immigrants, and almost all of those immigrants were men. In the next two decades the population of the city trebled. With men outnumbering women to such a huge degree, the brothels did a roaring trade.

At busy times, any good brothel would have a large number of men waiting while the girls were busy working, and most brothels employed musicians to keep the customers entertained while they waited. Just as in New Orleans, where brothels provided employment for early Jazz musicians who wouldn't have been able to get work anywhere else at that time, in Buenos Aires early Tango musicians got a chance of paid employment, which allowed them to develop their skills while playing for the waiting customers.

In a time before recorded sound, any live music was an opportunity to dance, and not to be missed. However, the reason the musicians were there was that the women were busy and the waiting men needed to be entertained, so the idea that the men were dancing with the women in the brothels is entirely fanciful. It is very likely that the women who worked in the brothels could dance the Tango, because they were for the most part working-class women and Tango was part of their culture. It is possible that at slow times the women might dance together to pass the time while waiting for clients. But it is very unlikely that the women would have danced with clients when they could be more profitably employed elsewhere.

At those busy times, since there was music to keep them entertained, the men would have danced with each other.

With women in such short supply in Buenos Aires, men who were interested in women had few options. One was to go to brothels. Another was to learn to dance the Tango as well as possible. Since it would be reasonable to assume that the men who frequented brothels tended to be men who were interested in women, it follows that they would have had an incentive to use the music provided to practise their dancing, so that, on the rare occasion that an opportunity presented itself of dancing with a woman, perhaps at a party in the patio of a *conventillo*, the tenement blocks that were the homes of the poor, they would be ready.

So when the men of letters walked into a brothel, as nineteenth-century men of letters sometimes did, they found there something that was completely alien to them – Tango music, which was never played at their own parties, and the dance, which their fashionable dance masters never taught them. It is no surprise, then, that in Argentinian literature Tango and brothels became tied together. The reality, though, is that, just as with Jazz, the brothels provided protection for a new art form that had emerged in a poor immigrant community, and that art form soon moved on to higher things.

There was, of course, a grey area. There were nightclubs where women were employed as hostesses, and part of the job was to dance with men. It was easy for commentators to assume that they also sold other services, and almost certainly some of them did. There were dime-a-dance halls, where 'lady teachers' would dance with men who gave them a ticket they had purchased at the door. And it was known that some women who worked in the sex industry chose to work as waitresses in cheap bars as a better way of picking up clients than walking the streets, and that some of these women would dance with men as a way of generating business. But these activities were normal everywhere in the world at the time. They were only associated with Tango in Buenos Aires because Tango was the dominant popular dance culture, and other industries made use of it. In other countries the same activities attached themselves to other dances, taking from the popular dance culture, but not contributing to it in any significant way.

The true home of Tango was the patio of a tenement block, where working-class Argentinians and recent immigrants from other countries met, mixed, played and danced together.

A Tango Timeline

The first recordings of Tango music were made in the first decade of the twentieth century. That makes the beginning of the twentieth century a good place to start a history of Tango, even though Tango had already been developing for several decades.

	Music	Song	Dance
Pre-1900	Early Tango	Early Tango	Early Tango
1900–1920	Period of transformation from early Tango to mature Tango.	Transformation from simple comic songs to complex poetic themes.	Worldwide Tangomania.
1920–1935	Classically trained musicians playing Tango. Music not necessarily aimed at the dance floor.	Tango in Buenos Aires dominated by star singers, who do not create music with dancers in mind.	As less dance music is played and recorded by Tango orchestras, fewer people dance.
1935–1955 The Golden Age of Tango	Innovative and challenging music aimed at the dance floor.	Great lyricists writing for singers who perform as an instrument in a dance band.	The most choreographically complex period of Tango dance history. Tango dance dominates the culture of Buenos Aires.
1955–1983 The Dark Age	Almost no work for bands playing for dancers. Many musicians leave Tango, or play only for shows.	Star singers dominate again.	The social dance driven underground. Tango stage and television shows start to use dancers who don't know how to dance the social dance.
1983 onwards The Tango Renaissance	A new market for Tango dance music, and also for show music and Tango fusion music of different kinds.	Increasing opportunities for singers to sing with dance bands again.	Tango danced all over the world again.

Tango Song and Tango Poetry

While in the English-speaking world we think of Tango as a dance, and tend to assume that the music will be instrumental, in the Spanish-speaking world many people come to Tango for the beauty of its lyrics.

In the first decade of the twentieth century, before Tango had reached musical and lyrical maturity, Tango songs were generally designed to be performed by music-hall artists, and were almost always comic, and often bawdy. They were frequently written in the first person, describing a character who told a story about what a great person he or she was – perhaps a dancer who could make women swoon across the city, or a ne'er-do-well who could get money without the inconvenience of work. They might comment on the innovations of the day – electricity, bicycles, the latest fashions. One of the two most instantly recognisable tangos ever written, *El Choclo*, was composed by Angel Villoldo for his own music hall act. *Choclo* means corncob, though in his lyric Villoldo was clearly using it as a euphemism for comic (and rather vulgar) effect. Whatever the subject of Tango songs at this time, the tone was always light-hearted.

In 1917 one of the most popular folk singers in Buenos Aires, Carlos Gardel, decided to record a tango for the first time. He chose a song called *Mi Noche Triste* – my sad night. It was the story of an abandoned lover, and had probably been intended as a comedy song, but Gardel sang it with all the tragedy of a broken heart. Although that recording was not an instant hit, other singers took note. Gardel had sensed a cultural change, and his gamble on the Tango would bring him colossal fame, not just in Argentina, but throughout the Spanish-speaking world.

Far away from Argentina, first Paris and then the rest of the northern hemisphere had been gripped by a massive Tangomania in the two years before the First World War. The popularity of Tango abroad meant that the middle and upper classes in Argentina, to whom Tango had previously been alien, and sometimes frightening, began to take an interest in it. The dance was still considered vulgar. The music, however, could enter the cultural mainstream more easily. Gardel had realised that there was the possibility of an audience for Tango music that did not want to dance, and that wanted sentimental entertainment rather than the raucous hilarity of the music hall.

Gardel (left) in 1915 with folk singer Razzano

This was the birth of serious Tango songs with serious lyrics. Following in the spirit of *Mi Noche Triste*, the subject of these songs was often unhappy love affairs. This was not the only theme, though, by any means.

One interesting theme shared by a number of songs is the warning to a young girl not to become a Tango dancer, not to go to the centre of Buenos Aires, and not to get involved with rich men who might give her presents, but to stay as close to home as possible and marry the poor boy next door. The theme is common enough to suggest that the temptation for women to do just that must have been great.

Another theme is praise of a loving mother, often one who has passed away. The singer may regret abandoning his mother, usually to run off with some woman who turned out to be wicked. This may have been a reflection of the guilt felt by some immigrants at having left their family behind, and of their sadness at never being able to see their parents again.

Sometimes the lyrics are philosophical. Sometimes they may be comic, or deal with unexpected themes like football – the other Argentinian obsession.

And Tango itself became an increasingly common theme.

Happy love songs are rare. Those that exist often contain some qualification – 'I am no longer made sad by the betrayal of my previous girlfriend now that I have you'. And that betrayal itself, in many different forms, was the dominant theme of Tango song.

The standard of the poetry of Tango lyrics was very high. Gifted writers found many ways to express passion and pain, in a manner that is very cathartic to the listener. Painful lyrics might be married to quite cheerful music, particularly in recordings aimed at the dance floor, allowing the singer to play with the emotions in a way that could be at once subtle and powerful.

With wonderful songs being written, constantly improving recording quality, the increasing popularity of radio, and the introduction of sound film, singers became the stars of the Tango, and in the late 1920s and early 1930s frequently had a fan base that did not dance, or was not dancing, but was listening to the radio or going to the movies instead.

Orchestras started playing arrangements designed to let the singer shine. These arrangements became less and less interesting to dance. As the music became less interesting to dance, people danced less, and the market for dance music diminished.

For a decade, from the mid-1920s to the mid-1930s, Tango song dominated the popular culture of Buenos Aires, and the dance slipped out of the limelight. It would take the return of the dancers in 1935 to bring Tango back into balance, releasing the energy that launched the Golden Age.

The Evolution of Tango Music

We do not know exactly what Tango music sounded like in the late nineteenth century. We know that the earliest Tango bands were made up of whatever instruments people had to hand, but that the preferred line-up seems to have been flute, violin and guitar. The earliest Tango sound recordings, which go back to the first decade of the twentieth century, suggest that nineteenth-century Tango had a distinctly Spanish feel, quite different from the sound we associate with Tango today (although, unusually for dance music, it shared with twentieth-century Tango the absence of a drum section). As Tango recordings first began to be made, that Spanish feel was already starting to disappear.

Buenos Aires at the beginning of the nineteenth century was a small town in a remote corner of the Spanish Empire. Its population was mostly of Spanish origin, often intermarried with the Native American population that had lived in the area before the arrival of Europeans, with a community of people of African origin who had arrived as slaves. This was the city in which the very earliest form of Tango appeared.

The avalanche of immigration into Argentina began in the middle of the nineteenth century, and by the 1890s the original population of Buenos Aires had been completely swamped by recent immigrants. Many of those immigrants came from Spain, but more came from Italy, and many of the Italians came from Naples – so many that the Buenos Aires slang word for Italian is *tano*, short for *napolitano*. The minority who were not Italian or Spanish almost all came from other parts of Europe.

Neapolitan song became a major influence on the developing Tango. Italian violinists brought a new lyrical beauty to Tango melody and the Tango began to become smoother and slower.

It was not only the influence of the Neapolitan violins that changed the nature of Tango at that time. Perhaps the most important newcomer of all was the bandoneon.

The bandoneon could be described as the instrument of torture, as it is one of the hardest instruments in the world to learn to play. It was originally designed to be a portable substitute for a church organ, with which it shares the complex, almost human quality of the sound produced by air flowing over its reeds.

It looks like a large concertina, with a button keyboard at each side. While people who can play it claim that the placement of the different notes on the keyboard makes practical sense, to the newcomer there appears to be no logic. Not only do the two keyboards not resemble each other, but each button plays a different note depending on whether the instrument is being pulled out or pushed in, with no apparent logical connection between them.

Such a difficult instrument to play would undoubtedly have disappeared, were it not for the fact that the sound it produces is unique. An accordion is simply not the same. Only the bandoneon has the catch in its throat that speaks of heartache. Nothing but the bandoneon produces the almost tactile sensation created in the listener when a skilled player plays a fast variation.

And only the bandoneon would do for the Tango.

By 1912, when Tangomania began in Paris, the bandoneon had already become established as the key Tango instrument, and the new, more lyrical, more tragic sound of the Tango had started to take root. The standard Tango orchestra, a sextet of two bandoneons, two violins, a piano and a double bass, became the norm. By 1920 Tango music was almost unrecognisably different from the music represented in the earliest Tango recordings, made little more than a decade earlier. It had become the music we know as Tango today.

The earliest Tango musicians, as is common for musicians in any form

A Bandoneon played by José Libertella

of popular music, tended to be amateurs with little, if any, training. The oldest Tango to remain in the repertoire today, *El Entrerriano*, written in 1897, survived in part because its composer, Rosendo Mendizabal, came from a middle-class background and could read music, so he could write his composition down.

As the Tango matured, musicians interested in Tango began to take classes both in playing and in composition. And musicians with classical training started to be attracted to the Tango.

Julio and Francisco De Caro learned to play violin and piano in the music school run by their father, who had been brought to Buenos Aires from La Scala, Milan. An ambitious man, he wanted his sons to be professionals. When Francisco, the older of the two, told his father that he wanted to be a Tango musician, his father threw him out of the house. Julio started sneaking out at night to listen to Tango orchestras, and was soon playing with giant of the early Tango Eduardo Arolas. When his father found out, he threw Julio out as well, and father and son did not speak to each other for over twenty years.

In 1923 the brothers began playing together in an orchestra run by Julio, and they continued to play together until Julio retired in 1953. They came to the Tango not out of a desire to improve it, but out of a passionate need to play the Tango as they heard it, in the best way they could. Their influence on all the Tango musicians who followed them was enormous.

During the late 1920s and early 1930s Tango arrangements started to develop a greater complexity, and the sound of the sextet began to take on some of the qualities of chamber music, with each instrument taking its own solo line.

The dancers, though, had drifted away.

In 1935 everything changed.

Violinist Juan D'Arienzo had discovered early in his career that he had more talent as an orchestra leader than as a musician, and gave up playing to conduct. His orchestra was doing reasonably well, and though they still didn't have a recording contract, they were the regular band at a nightclub in Buenos Aires.

The band played their first set fairly early in the evening, at a time when there were few, if any, customers. D'Arienzo sometimes didn't come in for the first set himself, and one particularly quiet evening when only the staff were there, instead of playing the usual arrangements, the band started to jam. The pianist, Rodolfo Biagi, began to play with a crisp, clean, foot-tapping rhythm, and an energy that had been missing in the Tango for over a decade. The staff of the nightclub loved it.

Later that evening when the club was busier and D'Arienzo had arrived, the band started to play their normal set. The staff of the nightclub requested a particular tune, and D'Arienzo began to conduct it. The staff objected – they wanted to hear it played the way the band had played it earlier that evening. D'Arienzo had a reputation for being extremely strict – even a note out of place would be punished – so the band was reluctant to let him hear how far they had strayed from the arrangement. But as soon as he heard the new sound inspired by Biagi's highly individual piano playing, and saw the reaction of the audience, he immediately adopted it as the sound of the orchestra, and never deviated from it through the rest of his long career.

It was not long before the orchestra got a recording contract, and they were an instant hit.

The new sound was not without its critics. Some saw it as a step backwards musically, and predicted that the orchestra's success would not outlast the summer. But the impact of D'Arienzo's orchestra was huge. The infectious rhythm drew people back to the dance floor in a way that even a few months earlier no one would have predicted.

The Golden Age had begun.

The Evolution of Tango Dance

Dance is more ephemeral than music and harder to record. Where video exists, the nature of the medium means that it does not show the reality of what was happening within the couple, distorting the apparent relationship between the bodies. And until very recently, in Buenos Aires the dance was not considered worthy of serious academic study.

Films made in Argentina in the 1930s and 1940s almost never show Tango as it was really danced. A character who dances is often a comic character, and Tango dance sequences are frequently staged in a way that has little to do with the genuine social dance.

This may be partly because the dance itself was a phenomenon of Buenos Aires, and not an important part of the culture elsewhere in the country or in the rest of the Spanish-speaking world, which provided the market for these films. The singers, though, had universal appeal, and Tango films tended to concentrate on them.

With little recorded evidence to go on, it is hard to reach back with any confidence to what the dance was like before 1940 – few of the dancers I met who were still dancing in the 1990s had begun to dance earlier than that.

What evidence we do have of Tango at the beginning of the twentieth century comes from a slightly surprising source. Tangomania in the northern hemisphere brought with it a hunger for information about the dance, and a variety of articles and books appeared. Little that was published at that time is reliable. Often a little bit of Tango is mixed with bits of other dances like the Brazilian Maxixe, forerunner of the Samba, or with the author's own inventions. Occasionally, though, a work like *Secrets of the Tango* by Samuel Beach Chester, with steps by an Argentinian dancer known as Juan Barrasa, seems to be an honest attempt by someone who actually knew how to dance the Tango to record something of its essence as a way of combating the misinformation coming from all sides.

We know that early Tango in Buenos Aires involved *cortes* – cuts – because we know they were banned from the better dance floors. Descriptions of a step called 'El Corte' recorded in the northern hemisphere suggest that it was a step in which the leader made a sudden sharp movement back, against the direction of flow around the dance floor, and that this might be done several times in succession. Certainly, that would be a good reason to ban it! Sudden sharp movements against the line of dance can be dangerous on a crowded dance floor.

In this step the sudden movement backwards is preceded by a small double-time weight change, also found in other steps recorded in the northern hemisphere at the time of Tangomania. This is a movement that sits very comfortably in the rhythm of Tango recordings from the period.

The descriptions of the corte recorded in the northern hemisphere at that time, along with the double-time weight changes in this and other steps, seem consistent with things I was shown when I asked dancers from the Golden Age how they remembered their parents and grandparents dancing when they were young.

The corte, as it was danced during Tangomania

If we can assume, then, that the more reliable documents written at the time of Tangomania do reflect something about the dance as it was done in Buenos Aires at that time, we can conclude that the position in which Tango was danced was the same as the position used during the Golden Age.

The two dancers stood directly in front of each other. They were not in the slightly offset position that would be adopted by Ballroom dancers of the next generation as they created the Foxtrot and the other Modern Ballroom dances.

So while the steps and the rhythm of the dance were a little different from those used in Buenos Aires in the 1940s, the technique may have been similar. It is possible to do the corte, and other steps suggested by these documents, with Golden Age technique (I have done so) – though that certainly does not prove that that is how they were done at the time. Still, since Tango steps in the Golden Age spring from the relationship between the two dancers and the music, rather than the other way around, it feels natural that a technique similar to the one used in the Golden Age coupled with the music of early Tango could give rise to the steps recorded at the time.

Changes to the Music Change the Dance

The change which took place in Tango music in the period up to 1920 must have had a great effect on the dance. The change in the rhythm, from the heartbeat-like rhythm of the earliest recordings (see *dos por cuatro* in Appendix 2: Some Tango Terms Explained) to the squarer rhythm of mature Tango, reduced the musical impulse for the double-time weight changes that seem to have been characteristic of the early dance. How exactly the dance changed at the time, and how long it took for dancers to adapt to the new rhythm, is something of which no record remains.

It seems to have been at the beginning of the Golden Age, in the mid-1930s, that the cross appeared. Without the cross, there could be no salida as we understand it. Early Tango seems to have contained a lot of sideways movement and turning. One very elderly woman told me that in the mid-1930s the woman started to spend more of her time in the dance walking backwards (and that she had never liked the change). That is consistent with this being the time when the salida appeared.

Golden Age dancers told me that their parents' generation did not always approve of their choreographic innovations, and 'dancing with the cross' was often mentioned.

Whether the technique used by Golden Age dancers went back to the very earliest form of Tango dance, or whether the Golden Age dancers refined and improved on Tango technique, is impossible to say. Over the course of the second half of the 1930s the number of people dancing increased, and, as happens with any burst of energy in any creative form, there were innovations. Just as the music became more refined and complex, the choreographic possibilities of the dance became deeper and richer.

Music, Song and Dance in the Golden Age

Historians of Tango generally agree that what made the Golden Age so extraordinary was the fact that all the branches of Tango were working together. This created a synergy and an excitement that raised standards in every area to a level that has never been matched before or since.

The most important market for Tango music was once again the market for dance music. The level of professionalism and aspiration of Tango musicians was much higher than it had ever been, so while creating music designed for the dance floor, they were able to add complexity to their arrangements that in turn fuelled the imagination and creativity of the dancers.

Singers also began to sing with the dancers in mind, performing as another instrument in the orchestra. The great singers of the period used the discipline of staying within the music as a means of intensifying the emotional content of their performance, and their subtlety also served as inspiration for the dancers.

Many new orchestras emerged, each with its own distinctive sound. Some, like D'Arienzo, stuck to a straightforward, crowd-pleasing style. Others combined the inspiration of innovators like the De Caro brothers with the energy provided by the dance floor, pushing the boundaries of the possible.

In the same way that many new sounds were created by the flourishing orchestras, many styles appeared in the dance. To the casual observer not experienced in the dance, those styles might look quite different, giving the impression that anything goes in Tango. That was not the case. All dancers danced in this period with the same technique, and it was the technique that defined what Tango was. How they chose to use that technique to trace shapes on the floor as they moved around it (the superficial expression of the dance that is all that the casual observer sees) varied enormously.

The spectrum of styles in the 1940s varied from the most elegant and restrained in the northern part of Buenos Aires, to the cheekiest and wildest in the south. This reflected something in the city. The southern edge of the city was the traditional port of entry of immigrants. It was a rough, dangerous part of town, with La Boca and its docks at one end, and Mataderos and its abattoirs at the other. The northern edge of the city was where the rich tended to have their homes, and while the rich generally had little to do with the Tango, the Tango dancers who lived on this side of the city tended to prefer elegance and discipline to raucousness and display. Dancers in the south enjoyed ganchos and boleos (steps where the follower's foot is flicked into the air). Dancers in the north considered it improper for ladies to do those movements, and they would not be seen in the northern milongas.

The shapes that a couple would trace on the floor would also be different. Dancers in the north traced long, elegant lines, interrupted by a complex shape created by an interesting choreographic pattern. Dancers in the south tended to move across the floor in curves. While the salida danced in the north of the city drew almost a straight line, the salida danced in the south was the shape of a rather curly question mark.

The interpretation of the music was also different, with different orchestras preferred in different parts of the city. The northern dancers preferred the orchestra of Carlos Di Sarli, whose clean, elegant musical lines suited their clean, elegant dancing. Southern dancers chose Osvaldo Pugliese, who consciously used the mechanical rhythms of the city to create a flexible, intense sound.

Each area of the city had its own style of the dance, just as each area of a large city tends to have its own subtly different accent. A knowledgeable person could locate a leader to the práctica he went to or his favourite milonga, just as a dialect expert can sometimes locate an accent to within a few streets.

Whenever I asked a dancer who had learned in the Golden Age what style they danced, they always answered 'Tango de Salón'. This was true whatever style they danced. If I asked them what they would call the style of another dancer who danced a different Golden Age style, they might try to find another way of describing it. But invariably that other dancer called their own style 'Tango de Salón', and might call the first dancer's style something else.

Underlying all that variation was a completely consistent technique. While, for example, dancers in the north tended to take longer steps than dancers in the south, the technique they used to take those steps was essentially the same. Style was superficial. Technique was the core of the dance.

There was no organisation deciding what correct technique should be and imposing it on dancers. The only explanation for the consistency of technique across all areas of the city, and all styles of choreographic expression, is that this was the technique that worked best. Either it was the technique that was already established when the Golden Age began, and no one who understood it found a way of improving on it, or any innovation that occurred in one part of town was quickly adopted and absorbed by all other dancers if it was better than the technique they already used. In as competitive an environment as Buenos Aires during the Golden Age of Tango, the best way of dancing would be the one everyone would adopt, and the level of technical skill shared by all dancers was very high.

Another style, often referred to by people who had been dancing in the 1940s as 'the style of the 1950s', seems to have been popular in a small number of milongas in the centre and south of Buenos Aires in the last years of the Golden Age. It was danced with short steps and relatively simple choreographic shapes, moving around the room in a manner that looks a little like Brownian motion. This style was ideally suited to small, crowded dance floors. Some Golden Age dancers I knew said they saw this style for the first time in the 1970s, when the few milongas they went to were often small, and the prácticas had disappeared encouraging a choreographically simpler form of the dance.

This style is characterised by its use of the ocho cortado. Dancers of this style always used the ocho cortado, never the forwards ocho. (see p.202) Dancers of other Golden Age styles always used the forwards ocho, never the ocho cortado. Anyone who dances both kinds of ocho is either a professional, or someone who learned to dance in the Tango Renaissance.

The ocho cortado – the cut ocho, or cut figure of eight step – is oddly reminiscent of the steps used at the time of Tangomania. Ocho cortado could be translated as 'ocho with a corte'.

Some dancers of other Golden Age styles thought of this style as a backward step in the development of Tango. One dear friend of mine from the north of the city struggled to find a way of describing the style that was suitable for the ears of a young lady, and finally chose, 'The style of a man who is looking for a girlfriend.' Of course, it would be possible to say that of almost any style of Tango, but what my friend was expressing was his sense that dancers of this style had abandoned the quest for the most evolved expression of Tango, and given in to the least demanding style, with motives that he could only assume were base.

While this style certainly was choreographically the simplest of the styles of the Golden Age, in some ways it was the purest, as it relied entirely on musicality and precise technique. Complex choreographic patterns can sometimes be used to hide flawed technique (not that the dancers of the Golden Age would ever have permitted that). Without flawless technique this style is nothing but a little low-impact aerobic exercise.

The style became highly influential in the Tango Renaissance in the 1990s, and was the inspiration for one of the new dance styles that appeared then.

The End of the Golden Age

In 1955 a military coup ousted Perón, the democratically elected president. The first junta was quickly ousted by another even more anti-Peronist dictatorship. It was the beginning of one of the bleakest periods of Argentina's history. The effects on the Tango were profound.

The Peronist government had actively encouraged Tango. As a

nationalist government, they chose to encourage anything that was identifiably Argentinian. Radio stations were only allowed to play limited amounts of music recorded in other countries. Naturally, this gave many opportunities to Tango artists. Some artists actively aligned themselves with the Peronist movement, particularly those involved with the musicians' union. (Unions were the backbone of the Peronist platform.) Tango was, after all, the culture of the working class, the section of society that Perón relied on for his support.

The new, anti-Peronist junta was immediately suspicious of anything supported by the Peronists. Also, the oligarchy in Argentina has traditionally tended to be Spanish, by both descent and inclination, and if not Spanish then British. (Many of the successful landowners and businessmen in Argentina were of British descent.) The working class in Buenos Aires were often descended from Italian immigrants, or were immigrants themselves. The cultures of the two groups were quite different, and to the members of the oligarchy who had now taken power, Tango was strange and alien.

Many prominent Tango artists found themselves either imprisoned or blacklisted for their Peronist associations – or even for the Peronist associations of their fans. And the junta actively encouraged the importation of the new popular music from the United States. Minors were not allowed into nightclubs, and this rule was actively enforced for Tango clubs but a blind eye was turned for clubs playing Rock and Roll. So 14- and 15-year-olds, instead of learning Tango as their older brothers and sisters had, were going to Rock and Roll clubs.

At various times in Buenos Aires meetings of more than two or three people were banned, and curfews were enforced, making it extremely difficult for any sort of social dance to take place.

This created a climate that forced the dance underground. Many people stopped dancing altogether. New people did not learn how to dance. While the dancing never stopped entirely, and there were always milongas open, they were hidden away and difficult to find.

Naturally, the market for orchestras playing for dancers withered.

Many musicians took to playing other styles of music. Some of the established orchestras continued to work, often touring in Japan.

Some work was available on the radio, and on the new medium of television. Without the discipline of playing for the dance floor, though, the music often tended towards the self-indulgent. The successful singers of this period have a more sentimental form of expression that is very different from the restrained passion of the great singers of the 1940s. Some of the best examples of Tango from this period are performed by artists who made their living playing other styles of music, and only performed Tango occasionally, out of love for the form.

It may be that Tango would have gone into decline even without the political upheaval that Argentina went through in those years. Rock and Roll became the culture of the young throughout the western world. Perhaps the prácticas would have started to disappear as older dancers got married and had children, leaving them without the time to go out dancing as often as they once had, and as younger dancers chose Rock and Roll as their way of meeting people. At around the same time, Ballroom dancing started to become less important in Britain, as other cultural avenues opened for the young, and that might have happened to the Tango in Argentina.

The last wave of immigration from Europe also ended at about the same time. Immediately after the Second World War many people left Italy, and other countries whose economies had been badly damaged in the conflict, looking for opportunities in the New World. The economic migration that had begun in the second half of the nineteenth century, bringing huge numbers of single men to Argentina, ended as the economies of Europe recovered from the war, while the Argentinian economy, based on agriculture rather than manufacturing, and compromised by politics, started to go into decline. Men no longer outnumbered women in the way they had in the first half of the twentieth century. The social forces that had created the práctica ceased to exist, so the práctica itself might have faded away, to be gradually replaced by different methods of passing on the Tango, which in turn might have changed the nature of the dance itself.

The political situation in Argentina, though, meant that the change was sudden. In Britain some people continued to learn to dance the Ballroom dances throughout the 1960s and 1970s, even though they were no longer part of the dominant popular culture of the young, so there is some continuity in the traditions of Ballroom dance. In Buenos Aires practically no one learned to dance the Tango for almost thirty years.

ONE NAME, MANY DANCES

Visions of Tango Outside Argentina

Tango was born in Argentina. There should be no need to say 'Argentinian Tango', because Tango is Argentinian. And yet for many people around the world the image that springs to mind on hearing the word Tango is of a dance that would never have been seen in Argentina.

There are many dances that bear the name Tango – French Tango, American Tango and Ballroom, International Style or Competitive Tango are the best known. None of these dances would exist had it not been for the Tangomania that swept the world in the years before the outbreak of the First World War.

The Tango Reaches Paris

Buenos Aires is a port city. Not only did this mean that it was a place where many different cultural influences mixed, it also meant that Argentinian sailors carried the culture of Buenos Aires to the other ports they visited. There is evidence that Tango was being danced occasionally in Marseille early in the twentieth century. Several Tango musicians went to France, and seemed somehow to be able to survive.

And there is also evidence of Tango being danced on stage in Montmartre in 1909.

But Tango's big breakthrough came in the salons of upper-class Paris in 1912.

In the early twentieth century the upper classes in Argentina were fabulously wealthy. Argentina had one of the world's largest and most successful economies, based on the export of agricultural produce. Rich Argentinians liked to educate their children well, and many were sent to Europe, either to study at university, or for a less formal education, doing the Grand Tour. A visit to Paris, seen by Argentina's elite as the cultural ideal, was a high priority. So in the years before the outbreak of the First World War, many rich young Argentinians became part of Paris society.

Tango in Argentina was a phenomenon of the urban working class. In the homes of the wealthy it was quite unknown. In their homes – but the teenage sons of the rich are not always in their parents' home. And somehow, quite a few of the young men who found their way into the most elegant salons in Paris had acquired the skill of dancing the Tango well enough to delight their Parisian hostesses. One can only imagine how very, very distressed the mothers of these young men would have been to discover this.

In the same way that Jazz shook off its disreputable image and became the music of the sophisticated by leaving New Orleans and arriving in New York or Chicago, far from the patios of the tenement blocks in Buenos Aires Tango became chic. The stage was set for one of the most extraordinary phenomena of early mass communication – Tangomania.

Tangomania

It is hard to appreciate the scale of the Tango fever that swept through the entire northern hemisphere in the two years before the outbreak of the First World War. The German Kaiser decreed that any officer caught dancing the Tango in uniform would be court-martialled. The Russian Tsar hired an Argentinian couple to teach the dance to his family. The Pope was urged to ban the dance, and asked to see a couple performing it. They danced very carefully, leaving him wondering what the fuss was about (he said it didn't look as much fun as the folk dance from the village where he was born), but preventing the ban. In all the great cities of Europe, and from New York to Shanghai and beyond, Tango became an obsession.

Anything could be sold by attaching the word Tango to it, and there are many advertisements from the period for Tango shoes, stockings, dresses and hats. Indeed fashion was changed by the mania for Tango. Feathers in ladies' hats were moved from their traditional horizontal sweep to the vertical position so associated with the 1920s in order to prevent the feathers from getting into the dance partner's eyes. Skirts became softer, and wrap skirts were invented, allowing freedom of movement for the legs. It is said that in Paris ladies even removed their corsets in order to dance the Tango.

Why did Tango take such a powerful hold on culture around the world? One reason was a taste for exoticism (which had also played a part in the success of Diaghilev's Ballets Russes at around the same time). But the Tango also represented something quite revolutionary in the world of social dance, at a time when dance still formed the backbone of social interaction in our culture.

Up until the twentieth century, social dance in the European tradition had been sequence dance. Whether at a ball or in a village square, with the occasional rare exception, everyone dancing to the same music would be dancing the same sequence of steps at the same time. Dance masters made a living teaching the sequences to those who could afford to learn. Sequence dances of this kind that are still danced today include the Scottish Country Dances, and some of the dances danced in Old Time Ballroom competitions.

At the end of the eighteenth century a folk dance from the Austrian countryside became fashionable in Vienna. This dance had a relatively short and simple sequence. In its folk dance form, a man put his arms around a woman's waist, she put her arms around his neck, and they whirled around in circles to music in three time. By the early nineteenth century this sequence had been formalised and had become what we now call the Viennese Waltz.

The idea of a man and a woman facing each other with their arms around each other, in public, while they danced, was revolutionary and very shocking, and so it took some time for the Waltz to become accepted.

As part of the formalisation of the Waltz in the early nineteenth century, the way in which the man and woman held each other was also formalised to make it seem less scandalous. The man lifted his left arm from the woman's waist, and she took hold of his left hand with her right (possibly to allow space for the hilt of an officer's sword worn formally at a ball, hanging at his left hip – something that had not been a problem for the peasants who had invented the dance).

This was the invention of the hold used in all modern couple dance today.

The Waltz – the first dance to use this hold – became fashionable across Europe in the 1830s, and continued to be the most important social dance in the upper levels of European society until the arrival of the Tango. (The more conventional kind of sequence dances remained popular across the rest of the social spectrum.) The Waltz was soon followed by another turning dance with a very simple sequence – the Polka.

Tango was only the third dance to use the revolutionary new hold.

But Tango did something that the Waltz and the Polka did not. It allowed different couples on the dance floor to do different things to the same music, creating the concept of leading and following in a social dance. In doing so it defined an entirely new kind of relationship between two people on the dance floor.

In order to make this possible, the Tango required a kind of physical intimacy that was completely new. This was combined with an unprecedented opportunity for creativity and beauty on the dance floor. Even now, a century later, these qualities in the Tango lead people to become obsessed with it. In the Europe of 1912 it was unlike anything anyone had ever seen before.

Argentinian dancers and musicians travelled to Europe and elsewhere to perform. They were not, however, the only influence on the development of the Tango in the northern hemisphere. There were Brazilian dancers who performed a dance called the Maxixe, which was often referred to as the Brazilian Tango (partly because people found it hard to pronounce its real name – *mashi'she* – and partly because the Tango was so fashionable), and Maxixe steps became mixed with Tango steps. There were also European and American dance teachers who added their own take on the dance.

When the First World War broke out, everything changed. Many of the Argentinian performers went home. The demand on the dance floor was for something simpler that soldiers home on leave could do without going to classes first. That gap was filled by the earliest form of the Foxtrot, which at the time was no more than walking round the room in time to fast music. (The Foxtrot would later become a much more complex dance, using as its basic step a variation of a pre-First World War Tango step.)

After the end of the War, the fashion for Tango returned, though not with the same intensity. Valentino's breakthrough performance, as a rich young Argentinian arriving in Paris in the years before the First World War and dancing the Tango with Parisian women in *The Four Horsemen of the Apocalypse* (1921), made him a star, and went a long way towards bringing the Tango back into fashion. Argentinian musicians toured Europe again, bringing the new Tango sound from Buenos Aires, and the smoother style was quickly adopted.

The Fragmentation of the Tango

Although Argentinian dancers and musicians performed, and sometimes taught, in Europe and America, many other people also found there was a good living to be made teaching and performing what they claimed to be authentic Tango. In 1914, Samuel Beach Chester, in his book *Secrets of the Tango*, described the situation in London at the time:

> [T]he essence of the new dance must have in it a great spark of vitality, to judge from the flaming, torch-lit conflagration which literally burns the world. With such a giant fire, many teachers of Tango dancing have sprung up like firemen, and, since they do not know the dance themselves, they cannot teach it; like firemen, therefore, they extinguish – enthusiasm, hope, or whatever the emotion may be . . .
>
> These people swarm in the West End now, and their ignorance of the Argentine Tango, in which they profess to be experts, is grotesque, ludicrous, to the Argentinos I have chanced to talk with. Their academic audacity is supreme, for each of these soi-disant authorities on the Tango claims a knowledge conflicting in every detail with the actual dance. One said to me: 'I wish to disassociate myself entirely with the Tango taught by all other teachers. Mine is the only correct Tango.' Whether this person hailed from Brixton or Barnsbury I do not know. I did not wait to ask! The Tango has given the brazen an opportunity to scream their wares from obscurity, and in a country over-full of amiable and credulous people they are able to make hay while the sun shines.

Wherever Tangomania took hold the same problems appeared. Vernon and Irene Castle, in their book *Modern Dancing*, warn those who would like to learn to dance the Tango to be careful in their selection of a teacher:

> American teachers go abroad for a few weeks, take a few lessons in the Abaye or some of the other places which live on the American tourist, come back home, and, having forgotten all they learned coming over, start in teaching. There are others who go to one of our seaside towns, such as Narragansett, and read of a new dance and begin teaching it. There is, unfortunately, no way of stopping these people. You can only pay your twenty five dollars an hour. If you don't learn the dance, you get a little exercise and a lot of experience.

It was inevitable under these circumstances that new dances would start to develop, even though they might continue to use the name 'Tango'.

The style of Tango that developed in Europe during Tangomania was often referred to as French Tango, and teachers in other countries would advertise the fact that they had recently returned from Paris with the latest Tango steps. Even in Buenos Aires, middle- and upper-class Argentinians were introduced to this new dance, and guides on how to do it were published specifically saying that this was the elegant dance done in the best salons in Paris, and had nothing to do with the coarse and disreputable dance done by the poor in their own city.

The Origin of Ballroom Tango

Through the 1920s and 1930s a number of popular dances developed in Britain, and came to be known as the Modern Ballroom dances. These are the dances seen throughout the world today in Ballroom competitions – Foxtrot, Quickstep, Waltz and Ballroom Tango.

Professional Ballroom teachers were concerned about the fact that a situation was developing where students who went to one teacher might find they could not dance with students who went to a different teacher. Hoping to ensure consistency from school to school, and also to improve the general level of technique, British dance teachers began to organise conferences to decide on a syllabus for each dance, so that all beginners could be guaranteed they would be learning the same steps wherever they went. The first conference in 1920 defined a syllabus for Tango that was essentially the French Tango of the pre-war period.

During the 1920s Argentinian Tango orchestras continued to play frequently in venues such as the Savoy Hotel in London. In 1922, aware of the smoother Tango now being danced in France under the influence of the smoother music coming from Argentina, the British Ballroom teachers invited a teacher from Paris to demonstrate the new French style to another conference, and a modified syllabus was adopted. This syllabus continued unchanged into the late 1930s.

In the meantime, the Foxtrot was being transformed from a simple dance in which a couple just walked round the room in time to quick music, into a dance that was slower, more elegant and more complex. It absorbed many qualities from the Tango. Even its basic step is an adaptation of a Tango step danced before the First World War. In the early 1930s there was a brief vogue for a hybrid known as the Tango Foxtrot, and it is quite possible that in time the Ballroom community might have absorbed Tango into the Foxtrot completely, in the same way that the Charleston was absorbed into the Quickstep. (The original full name of the Quickstep was the 'Quick Time Foxtrot and Charleston'.)

In 1933 a German Ballroom dancer called Freddie Camp, who competed as an amateur, moved to London. He had a distinctive and personal style of Tango. Freddie Camp invented the sharp, staccato movements and the flick of the head from side to side that so characterise Ballroom Tango as we know it today. (These movements were never done by Tango dancers in Argentina.)

He and his partner, Alida Pasqual, appeared for the first time in the Blackpool competition – then, as now, the most important Ballroom competition in the world – in 1935. In his personal memoir of the Blackpool competition from 1931 to 1978, *Blackpool, My Blackpool*, Kit Hallewell describes the experience of seeing this style of Tango for the first time:

> The year's British Amateur was set alight when there burst upon Blackpool the sensation of Freddie Camp's Tango . . . Freddie's Tango was certainly revolutionary. Its main characteristic lay in the explosion of vigorous action from stillness. And the body stillness was itself instinct with the expectation of the next action. He had this ability to rivet the spectator's attention in this expectation, and when the action came the crowd rose to it . . . Freddie Camp was the innovator and archetype of the new Tango.

Some commentators assumed, since Camp was German, that this was the German style of Tango, though Camp himself denied it. He wrote in the magazine *The Modern Dance* in May 1936:

> I would like to state that there is nothing German in our dance as far as interpretation of rhythm and style is concerned, but that it is entirely our own creation.

And, describing the creation of that style, he said:

> A few years ago, when dancing the Tango on the Continent in the style which had been popular for a long time, I discovered that I danced to the melody only and not to the rhythm of the dance. This did not satisfy me . . . I came to the conclusion that it would be more natural to dance it in a more rhythmic way.

Camp's comment about changing from dancing the melody to dancing the rhythm is an interesting one. In Argentina dancers prided themselves on their ability to dance the melody rather than the rhythm. Indeed, Tango orchestras almost never have a drum section. While most other dance music around the world is based on a strong, clear rhythm, generally emphasised by drums, newcomers to Tango music often complain that they find the rhythm of the music difficult to hear. This is one of the qualities that makes Argentinian Tango unique.

Camp's staccato Tango, with its emphasis on rhythm rather than melody, was also more flamboyant and spectacular than the existing style, which started to be called 'traditional', 'soft' or 'smooth'. Not all commentators were immediately won over by the new style. Monsieur Pierre, a French dancer who had arrived in London during Tangomania, and had been a successful dance teacher for more than two decades, said, again in *The Modern Dance*, that he liked the idea of the staccato Tango, but thought it was being taken too far. He felt that competitive dancers used the staccato movements in order to catch the judges' eye, and performers used it to generate applause, but that neither could really enjoy dancing in that way. He said,

> I believe that if competitions and demonstrations were suddenly to stop, the staccato Tango would not last another week!

In an interview in the same magazine in June 1936, Walford Hayden, a band leader well known at the time for his frequent appearances on the BBC, put his objections more firmly:

> Dance these adaptations if you like . . . but don't call this bastardised form by its original name – give it a new one.

However, these dissenting voices were out of step with the times. Competitions and demonstrations did not suddenly stop, and the more flamboyant staccato Tango did not disappear, but only increased in popularity.

Freddie Camp competed as an amateur, so was not allowed to teach. Professional teachers began taking out advertisements saying that they taught Tango in Camp's style – a unique tribute to the achievement of a unique dancer – and the style quickly spread around the country.

Around the same time Victor Silvester began to record dance music. He had trained as a musician, and had then been a champion Ballroom dancer for many years before starting his own orchestra. His musical philosophy was that complex arrangements were wasted on the dance floor, and that what dancers really needed was a melody over a strict tempo rhythm – the opposite approach from that taken by the Tango orchestras in Buenos Aires in the Golden Age. His dance-music recordings were enormously successful, and are still considered by some Ballroom dancers to be the best ever made. The emphasis on rhythm is similar to Camp's approach to the Tango, and the two innovations must have reinforced each other.

Ballroom Tango music became more rhythmic, and the snare drum or military drum was added to emphasise the rhythm even further. The staccato style increased in popularity, and the 'soft' Tango soon disappeared. Ballroom Tango had become a dance in its own right, with its own music and its own personality, completely different from the Argentinian dance.

Freddie Camp is said to have gone into the Pioneer Corps when the Second World War began. He was never seen in the Ballroom world again.

The Origin of American Tango

American Tango owes a great deal of its character to Vernon and Irene Castle.

The Castles began their careers as actors. They had their first success as dancers in Paris and returned to America in 1912, where they became famous as teachers and performers of social dance. Irene also became a leader of fashion, and was the first well-known American woman to cut her hair short. They visited Paris each year to perform, and it was in Paris that they learned to dance the Tango.

When the Tango first appeared in Europe, inevitably some people were shocked by the intimacy of the new dance. Controversy fanned the flames of Tangomania, seeming only to bring it greater success.

In the United States, though, the mood was different. The Prohibition movement was gaining momentum, and as well as trying to ban alcohol, many people wanted to ban social dance. The Castles begin their book *Modern Dancing* by saying that their purpose is to show 'that dancing, properly executed, is neither vulgar nor immodest, but, on the contrary, the personification of refinement, grace and modesty', and say repeatedly that dancing is good, hygienic exercise for young and old, that it encourages refinement, and that it is only vulgar when it is not done properly. They argue that better teaching is the way forward, not a ban.

Their approach to all the dances they taught was to clean them up and make them more acceptable to their home audience. They advocated a more open hold, saying they would prefer to see a return to

> the old rule that the man should touch only his partner's fingertips as they tread the measures of the dance. In this reconstruction the Tango will play its part; a sublimated form of the Tango, I admit, but still the Tango.

They said of their own Tango that it was 'much modified from the first Argentine', and they even created a dance they called the Innovation, which was exactly the same as their Tango, but with no physical contact between the two dancers at all.

The classic Tango scene from *The Four Horsemen of the Apocalypse* (1921) gives an interesting glimpse of the difference between American and European Tango at this time. Valentino had spent time in Paris during Tangomania, and had learned to dance the Tango there. He arrived in America in December 1913 and worked as a dancer before becoming an actor. Although his partner does not appear to be a skilled dancer, it is interesting to see the softness and sensuality of Valentino's dancing when compared to the less fluid dancing of the American extras in the background, dancing the Tango as they understood it. Little remains to show us what social dance was like at this time. This scene may not be the ideal recording of Tango in America in 1921, but it is a tantalising suggestion of what may have been happening on the dance floor.

THE TANGO RENAISSANCE

A New Beginning in Buenos Aires and Around the World

1983 was one of the most important years in the history of Argentina. It was the year when the military junta finally fell after the fiasco of the Falklands (Malvinas) War, and democracy returned. It was also a pivotal year in the history of Tango, with the premiere of the show *Tango Argentino* in Paris.

In Argentina, when the junta fell, there was a sudden burst of interest in dancing Tango. Tango represented something that was fundamentally Argentinian, and young people who had lived through a horrific period where their pride in their national identity had been stretched to the limits, could once again find joy in saying *'eso es lo nuestro'* – this is ours.

And pride in the Tango was given an enormous boost by the worldwide interest generated by the show *Tango Argentino*.

The show was created by the team of Claudio Segovia and Hector Orezzoli. When it opened in London it was described by *The Spectator* as 'a flawless work of art' and by the *Financial Times* as 'sexual, glamorous and fateful . . . this is the kind of vivid, meticulous, serious staging that we associate with Diaghilev'. Everywhere it played in the world, critics and audiences went wild.

And everywhere that *Tango Argentino* played, it left behind it a small but enthusiastic group of people determined to learn to dance the Tango.

The show's success was based on performances by the very best dancers of the day – many of whom had begun dancing in the last years of the Golden Age – music by the great Sexteto Major, with the addition of notable guest artists, and the unfailing good taste and passion of Segovia and Orezzoli, who pulled the performances of their lives from some of Argentina's most important artists.

Huge numbers of people began to learn to dance the Tango as a result of seeing the show. Many travelled to Buenos Aires, searching for teachers and for people who had been dancing during the Golden Age. And there began to be an active market for Tango teachers, principally in Europe, the United States and Japan, and also for Tango shows and Tango recordings.

Traditional Saturday night milonga at Sunderland Club, Buenos Aires, 2001

Gradually record companies began to re-release recordings from the Golden Age that had been unavailable for decades. Young musicians were inspired by these recordings, and by the dance craze. And once again, a market began to exist for bands that played for dancers.

How the New Generation Learned to Dance

In Buenos Aires the prácticas disappeared in the years after the 1955 coup. Outside Argentina, prácticas had never existed. The new generation of Tango dancers, both in Buenos Aires and around the world, did not have access to the traditional method of acquiring the skills of Tango.

Many of the people who learned to dance during the Golden Age had stopped going to milongas, often because they were married with children and simply didn't have time any more, but also because of the climate of fear that existed in Argentina through the 1970s. When the military junta fell in 1983, and democracy returned, many in the older generation remained nervous. The complicated political history of Argentina in the twentieth century meant they had seen brief spells of democracy before, which always seemed to be ended by another coup. And those who had continued to dance during the 1970s and early 1980s had no reason to welcome strangers. In those difficult times unfamiliar people might be there because they had been sent by the military to observe. Young people did not know how to dance the Tango, they reasoned, so why would a young person choose to go to a milonga? A friend of mine told me that when she first became interested in Tango she went to milongas regularly for several years before someone actually asked her to dance. (I might add that she is a very beautiful woman, making the fact that she was ignored even more remarkable.)

Even in the 1990s, a very few Golden Age dancers told me they felt more comfortable talking to me than they did to Argentinians they did not know well, because I was a foreigner, so they didn't have to worry about any potential consequences. If they felt they were starting to get to know the other regulars at a milonga, they would stop going there for a while, and try somewhere else where they didn't know anyone, so as to be able to keep their distance.

That was rare, but it shows an extreme of a general nervousness about talking to strangers that was quite understandable given Argentina's history.

So even though in the 1980s there were many people living in Buenos Aires who had learned to dance in the Golden Age, some of whom were going to milongas regularly, young people interested in learning to dance the Tango did not necessarily have easy access to them.

And those of us in Europe or the United States who wanted to learn to dance were thousands of miles away from the people who contained within their bodies the distilled wisdom of all the generations of Tango dancers who had gone before.

People with little knowledge of the history of Tango tend to assume that to learn to dance the Tango (or any other dance), the thing to do is to go to a beginners' class. At that beginners' class they assume that they will learn a step, which they will try to do with another beginner who has also just learned the step, and that then they will go to a dance and try and repeat that step with someone else who already knows it. Learning technique is not something many novices give much thought to, unless they are told that it is what they need to do.

At a beginners' class, and probably at a dance that follows it, they will be surrounded by other beginners. They rely on the teacher, and perhaps a small group of more advanced students, to give them the information they need about the dance, and put their faith in the assumption that the teacher must know what they are talking about, or they would not be teaching a class.

One of the fundamental differences between a class and a práctica as a way of passing on the dance is that in a group class the student generally receives the bulk of their information through the eyes and ears, and processes that information mentally in an attempt to communicate it to the body, while in a práctica the person learning receives information through the body, directly from the body of the more experienced dancer. In a class the student relies on the teacher having two skills – skill in the dance itself, plus the ability to communicate that skill in a way the student can comprehend. It was rare to find people who learned to dance in the prácticas of the Golden Age who had the ability to articulate and explain the highly developed skills in the dance that they possessed. Conversely, sometimes people who were skilled communicators, able to teach a class with conviction and confidence, did not have an equivalent level of skill in the dance, and might teach things that would not have been recognised by the dancers of the Golden Age – the dancers who represented the continuous, living tradition of Tango – as being Tango at all. It is a very fortunate student who finds a teacher who has true knowledge and understanding of the dance, as well as the skills to communicate that knowledge.

A friend of mine in Buenos Aires, who decided she wanted to learn the Tango in the early 1980s, like many another beginner, looked for a class. Because she was a trained dancer, she picked up the steps very quickly, and before long she was the teacher's assistant. After about eighteen months, out of curiosity, she decided to go to a milonga. She walked in, looked at the dancers, and instantly realised that what she had been learning for a year and a half had absolutely nothing to do with the Tango. She fled the milonga in floods of tears. Fortunately, she had both the insight to understand what had happened, and the determination to start again from scratch. She found Golden Age dancers to learn from, she worked hard, and she became a wonderful Tango dancer with beautiful technique, helping to carry forwards the tradition of the dancers of the Golden Age.

This may be an extreme, but it is not so very different from my own first experience of Tango, or the experience of others around the world.

Another common experience in the Tango Renaissance was one I had when people first started asking me to teach. It was not because I knew much about the Tango then – I certainly did not! – but because I knew a little more than they did. At that time I could not have begun to imagine how much I still had to learn about Tango. In Buenos Aires in the Golden Age a man would have gone to the práctica four or five times a week for three years before he was allowed to consider himself a good enough beginner to walk into his first milonga. People like me, well meaning and genuinely trying to be as true to the Tango as possible, were often trying to teach other people to dance after having been to only a few classes ourselves.

Some dancers tried to re-create the práctica experience by getting together to explore the dance. Frequently, though, the missing ingredient was a group of highly skilled dancers to dance with and learn from. Learning a language naturally can only happen if a child is exposed to people who speak the language fluently. A group of children deprived of adult contact will find a way of communicating with each other, but that way of communicating will not be English, Spanish or any other existing language. In a práctica, dancers can only pass on the skills they already have or discover together. The skills learned in the práctica will only be the essential technique of Tango if there are people there who already have, or are studying, that technique.

Fortunately in Buenos Aires in the 1980s and 1990s there were places where it was possible to learn from dancers who were part of the continuous, living tradition of Tango, going back to the Golden Age. Those who were searching for the Tango were able to find it. Those who wanted knowledge could find those with knowledge to give.

In the 1990s in Buenos Aires dancers who had learned to dance in the Golden Age and the new generation of dancers began to mix, which in practice mostly meant men who had learned in the prácticas dancing with young women. The new freedom allowed the younger generation of dancers far greater opportunities to learn from dancers of the Golden Age.

Possibilities for the young dancer gradually multiplied. There was a generation of young Tango teachers, some of whom had been dancing since the early 1980s, who had built a reputation and a following. There were teachers who began with an interest in stage choreographies, and who later started teaching people who wanted to learn the social dance. There were dancers of the Golden Age, both professionals and people who taught for love, who did their best to give what they knew to those with an interest in learning the Tango. And in the milongas the new dancers could dance not just with each other, but also with dancers who were part of the continuous, living tradition of Tango.

The 1990s were a thrilling time to be a Tango dancer.

Making eye contact in the Confitería Ideal, Buenos Aires, 2001

Fashions change in the new generation of dancers in Buenos Aires, and in the rest of the world. The early Tango Renaissance was dominated by complicated steps, often at the expense of technique. This is not surprising, as the steps are the easiest thing for a newcomer to see. Complicated steps are instantly appealing, especially to those with a dance background, or with a desire to perform.

In the 1990s there was a backlash against the complicated figures. Some people in the younger generation felt that people were using steps as a way of keeping at bay the intimate connection that Tango called for, and, indeed, there were those who did. A new style became fashionable, inspired by the choreographically pared-down style that some people who danced in the 1940s referred to as 'the style of the 1950s' which brought the connection between the partners and with the music into a sharper focus. This new style was given the name 'Estilo Milonguero'. Many people began to assume that this was the only authentic style of Tango in the Golden Age, although it was based on a style used by a minority of dancers at that time. When done well, this style is delightful, though it is not the whole story of Tango. And ironically, some young dancers have found a way of using the closer hold made popular by this style to keep their partner at a greater emotional distance, by changing the relationship between the hearts.

This style in turn generated a backlash from those who enjoyed the choreographic complexity that Tango had to offer, some of whom had been attracted to Tango by the excitement of stage performances they had seen, rather than by the experience of dancing with a skilled dancer. The idea that this pared-down style of Tango that had become popular was the *only* authentic social Tango style from the Golden Age left some who were looking for a greater choreographic challenge with the impression that complex Tango steps were a new invention. They assumed there was nothing to learn from the generations who had danced before. They turned to the Stage, to other dances, and to their own experiments for ideas. All dancers, of course, have something unique to add. And people do create choreographic patterns that they have never seen anyone else do. That does not mean, though, that other dancers have not already done them, and perhaps done them better. My own experience is that I could be saved many months of experimentation by a few minutes with a Golden Age dancer who already knew how to do the movement, and the result would invariably be better, as the Golden Age dancer's method was based on the experimentation of all the many generations of dancers who had gone before.

While fashions in the Tango scene may come and go, there always have been and always will be those whose love of Tango takes them beyond the surface to a deeper understanding of the true nature of the dance.

At the beginning of the twenty-first century there is a strong and vibrant Tango scene around the world. Today somewhere a highly skilled dancer is teaching a workshop, a Tango show is being performed, and in a small town someone is teaching their first ever Tango class, not because they think they know everything about the Tango, but because

Dancers of the new generation at Sunderland Club, Buenos Aires, 2001

they hope they know a little more than the other people around them, and they are doing what they can to help those others learn something about the reality of this extraordinary dance. Tango continues to capture the imagination in a way that no other dance does.

We also find ourselves at a turning point. The last great generation of dancers from the Golden Age is fading away. Even in Buenos Aires, it is no longer possible to go to a milonga and see a whole room full of people dancing as they danced then – an unforgettable sight to anyone who experienced it. We are the generation of dancers who will decide what Tango will be in the future.

PART III

Tango Technique
in the
Golden Age

THE ESSENCE OF TANGO TECHNIQUE

Trying to describe the technique used by dancers who danced the Tango in Buenos Aires during the Golden Age can make it seem very complicated. There are many details to get right if the dance is to work as the people who created it experienced it.

But it all becomes simple if the dancer remembers that the essence of good technique is to keep the two hearts perfectly together at all times throughout the dance, and that the purpose of this is to give the most satisfying dance to both partners, both emotionally and creatively. Good technique is designed to create an emotional connection, and also to create a framework that gives the maximum possible choreographic freedom.

Good technique takes time and effort to acquire. Learning a step may take an hour. Acquiring excellent technique may take years of practice – but it also makes learning new steps so easy that it becomes trivial.

The technique used in Buenos Aires in the Golden Age was the result of perhaps as much as a century of experimentation. Many generations of Tango dancers had refined and polished it. Each part of the technique was used because it gave a better experience to the people dancing than any alternative anyone had tried. It may be that better techniques will be developed in the future. We will only be able to tell if new techniques are better than the old ones if we know what the old techniques are.

Because of the discontinuity between 1955 and 1983, when almost no one learned to dance the Tango, our generation has the responsibility of being the bridge between the dancers of the Golden Age and future generations of Tango dancers. Only if we understand the techniques used by the Golden Age dancers can we be sure that what we are passing on to future generations is as good or better.

When I talk about keeping the hearts together, there are two things that I should clarify. First, to be anatomically correct, I am referring to the centre of the body at the level of the heart, rather than specifically the heart itself, which is slightly to one side. It would be more accurate to refer to the breastbone, but the word heart conveys the meaning much better.

Second, the hearts should be directly in front of each other, in the sense that the precise centres of the two bodies are aligned. If one dancer is taller than the other then the hearts will be separated vertically. This should not alter the fact that each dancer's focus is on the position of the other dancer's heart.

And from a mechanical point of view it may be useful to remember that the follower's centre of gravity is in the centre of the body directly below the heart. In moving the follower's heart, the leader is moving the follower's centre of gravity, therefore actually moving the follower's body – the leader is not giving signals that the follower needs to interpret. The relationship is direct, not coded.

Posture

The ideal posture for Tango is similar to the ideal posture for most physical activity. The torso is upright and vertical. The head is balanced on top of the spine. The body is relaxed.

The difference is that to dance the Tango, the knees are softened so that the torso is very slightly closer to the floor, and the weight is then carried forwards to the front of the foot. This brings the heart as close as possible to the partner, while still making it possible to stay completely in balance.

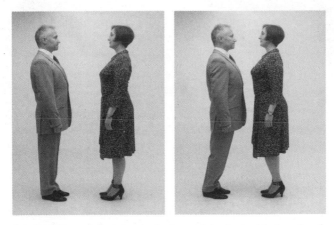

Bringing the weight towards the front of the foot while keeping the torso upright brings the hearts as close together as possible.

Technical skill	How this skill keeps the two hearts together
The torso is kept perfectly vertical, with the shoulders over the hips.	If the shoulders are slumped or the torso leans forwards, the head comes in front of the heart, pushing the partner away from the heart, and the heart away from the partner. Similarly, if the hips are pushed forwards or back the heart is pulled away from the partner. (When dancers dance together with correct technique there can be an optical illusion that gives the impression that they are leaning the torso forward rather than keeping it vertical. This illusion is caused by the use of the legs and the position of the weight.)
The knees are soft.	If the dancer stands on straight legs, then each time a step is taken the heart will be dropped, and then come up again as the dancer returns to the standing position, and this will tear apart the relationship between the two hearts. Keeping the knees soft allows the heart to stay constantly on the same level throughout the dance. If each heart stays on one level throughout the dance then it is far easier to keep the relationship between the two hearts constant. A dancer may attempt to compensate for a stiff leg by shifting the hip to the side (the technique used in some dances to create 'Latin hip action'). Shifting the hips in this way breaks the relationship between the dancer's heart and the dancer's foot. The foot can no longer hang passively from the heart and go where the heart goes. This in turn breaks the relationship between the two hearts, making it lack the softness and warmth sought by the Golden Age dancers.

The torso is moved forwards so that the weight is over the balls of the toes.	It would be possible for the dancer to stay in balance with the weight in the centre of the foot or even on the heel, but by sliding the weight forwards as far as it can go along the foot, while keeping the torso vertical, the dancer brings the heart as close to the partner as possible. This is made possible by the fact that the knees are soft, allowing the dancer to stay comfortably in balance while bringing the torso forwards.
The dancer stands with all of the weight on one leg. The other leg hangs passively by its side, allowing gravity to bring it next to the supporting leg.	This skill is particularly important for the follower, as it ensures that the correct leg is free at all times. The weight is only transferred from one leg to the other if the leader leads the change, not because the legs are brought together. If the follower places weight on both feet then it is much harder for the leader to lead the next step accurately, as the follower could move with either leg. Keeping the free leg hanging from the heart means it will go wherever the leader takes the heart. If the follower uses muscular strength to hold the legs together or to hold the weight off the free foot, that effort will prevent the leader from being able to lead either an extension or a transfer of weight that the follower is not expecting. For both dancers, having the free leg hanging from the heart allows the step forwards to be performed correctly – vital to keeping the hearts together. For the leader, having the weight on just one foot facilitates leading a transfer of weight correctly – one of the most delicate and subtle moves to lead and follow.

Although all of the weight is forwards on the balls of the toes of one foot, the heels stay in contact with the floor.	It is common for people, particularly those with a Ballet background, to hear that the weight is on the toes and assume that means the heels are lifted from the floor. This, however, introduces a tension into the leg that in turn creates a tension or stiffness in the torso and in the relationship between the hearts, which was not something the Golden Age dancers found pleasant. Resting the heels on the floor, albeit without weight, allows a relaxation of the leg that allows the leg more perfectly to follow the movement of the heart, and therefore allows the connection between the two dancers to be much warmer.
The shoulders and hips are kept horizontal at all times.	There is no hip action or rolling of the shoulders. Keeping the shoulders and hips in alignment at all times allows the leg to be controlled by the movement of the heart. Rocking the hips or shoulders breaks the connection between the heart and the leg. The legs must be moved by the movement of the heart if the relationship between the two dancers is to be correct.

Extending the Foot Back

A step back, whether it is for the leader or the follower, is made up of two parts. The first part is the extension of the foot back, without the heart moving back with it. The second is the movement of the heart, and with it the rest of the body. Learning to extend the foot back correctly is a fundamental skill. Without this skill the dancer will never be able to dance well.

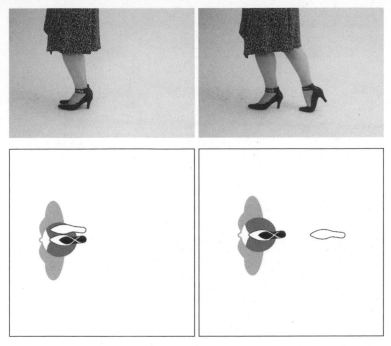

Extending the foot back

Although the foot moves back, the heart still has the sense of moving forwards. The heart is constantly searching for the heart of the partner, constantly trying to find a place within the partner's heart.

Technical skill	How this skill keeps the two hearts together
The foot extends straight back so that it is behind the supporting leg, along the line joining the two hearts, which is also perpendicular to the hips.	If each step back is taken with the weight-bearing part of the foot on the same line then the heart will travel on a straight line. If the foot is placed on either side of that line the heart will move from side to side with each step. That would tear apart the relationship between the two hearts (unless both hearts moved by exactly the same distance). By keeping both hearts travelling on

	one straight line – the line that joins the hearts – they can easily be kept in perfect unison.
The foot travels back just above the floor, not sliding along it.	In many dances the foot slides along the floor when it moves back. The friction created by the movement of the foot along the floor, no matter how smooth the floor may be, would, in Tango, disrupt the direct relationship between the foot and the heart, as it would introduce a force, albeit a small one, other than the action of gravity on the leg hanging from the heart. Only by moving just above the floor can the foot be placed with absolute precision.
The foot lands with the balls of the toes in contact with the floor, so that the toes are flat.	Having the toes flat on the floor gives a solid base ready to accept the dancer's weight as it is carried back over the foot. It is tempting to point the toes, as one might in Ballet, when extending the foot back. However, that would give no base for the weight to move onto, which would mean there was a moment when the dancer would be out of balance, and the dancer would fall onto the back foot. Having the toes flat means that the dancer is able to control the balance at all times, giving a greater degree of subtlety and control.
The toes are pointed directly forwards, directly at the partner's heart.	Turning the foot out at the moment of extension makes it harder to ensure that the heart travels on one straight line. It also requires muscular effort, which may interfere with the relationship between the foot and the heart. At the end of the step the foot would need to be turned to be in the correct position. By keeping the toes pointed at the partner's heart at all times, just as the heart is always pointed at the partner's heart, the focus is

	maintained, and there is no danger that the foot will be placed somewhere other than where the heart needs to go.
The ankle is extended so that the foot from the ankle to the balls of the toes is an extension of the lower leg.	This allows the maximum possible length of the extension, as well as giving a line to the leg that the dancers of the Golden Age found aesthetically pleasing. The longer the step back both dancers are capable of doing, the more flexibility the leader has in how long a step to lead. (That is not to say that the follower always takes the longest possible step back − that would be to ignore the leader's lead of the length of the extension. The follower needs to be technically capable of taking a long step, but when dancing must follow the length of the extension that the leader leads.)
The leg is extended back so it is almost straight, but the knee is not locked.	Extending the leg until it is almost straight allows the dancer to increase the potential length of the step. However, the knee must not be locked, as this would prevent the torso from moving back on one level during the transfer of weight to the back foot. For the follower, a straight leg could act almost like a flying buttress. The straight leg connected to the floor would apply a force against the leader carrying the follower's heart back − instead of simply moving the follower's heart, the leader would almost be trying to move the whole building. A straight leg would also force the follower's heart to rise, as it moved from its original angle towards the vertical.

	The follower's leg must be soft to allow it to fold as the leader moves the torso. The leader's leg must be soft so that the leader can stay on one level while moving the hearts.
For the follower, the length of the extension is led by the movement of the leader's heart directly through the follower's heart.	Although the dancer should practise exercises with the longest possible extension of the leg, given the other technical constraints and the dancer's own body, the follower should not always make the maximum extension when dancing, but should make the extension that the leader leads. It is the speed of motion of the leader's heart through the follower's heart at the moment of extension that leads the length of the step, sometimes described as the pressure that the leader's heart applies to the follower's heart. If the leader moves the follower's heart with greater speed then the distance covered in the course of the step will be greater. If the leader moves the follower's heart with less speed, the step will be shorter.
	This is not something the follower should try to analyse while dancing. The thought process would take too long, and the movement would be made too late. It is something the follower trains the body to feel, and that happens below the level of conscious thought
The follower places the foot on the music.	This is an important way in which the follower expresses musicality, but more than that, it helps the leader to know when one part of the step has been led and the next part can be begun. The follower places the foot exactly where the leader has carried it when the beat of the music arrives. If the follower places the foot earlier than that,

	then the foot may not have reached the point the leader expected. If the follower places the foot after the beat of the music, the leader will have assumed that the follower's foot had been placed and may have begun to try to lead the next movement. The follower's heart will have been carried in a new direction, so the follower's foot, being moved by the follower's heart, will arrive somewhere other than where the leader expected. The follower may end up on the wrong foot. The music is the third member of the couple, keeping the movements of the hearts and feet integrated.
The follower's foot, once placed, does not move again unless the leader leads it to return to the standing position.	The follower's foot has been placed where the leader placed it at the moment of extension. The follower should not make any adjustment to its position. It is where it is, and it is now the leader's job to deal with it. The leader's body is trained to know where the follower's foot has been placed, and the leader will be leading the next movement according to the reality of where the follower is. If the follower changes that reality, the follower invalidates the leader's lead.

Transferring the Weight Back

Learning to transfer the whole body back as one piece, with the front foot hanging from the heart, going wherever the heart is taken, is what separates the skilled follower from the novice. This skill opens the door to learning to step forwards correctly, as the step forwards is the reverse of the transfer back.

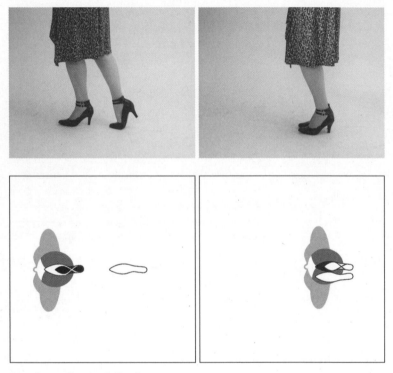

Transfering the weight back

The desire of the heart is always to be moving forwards, towards the partner's heart. When the heart is carried back it moves with some reluctance, staying as far forwards as it can. In this way the person stepping back does not step away from the partner. The intention is always towards the partner, even though the motion is back. The heart moves at the same speed as the partner's heart moves towards it, so the hearts remain united and still.

Technical skill	How this skill keeps the two hearts together
The torso moves smoothly back, with the heart staying at one level throughout.	If the heart moved up or down through the course of the movement of the torso, this would tear apart the relationship between the two hearts. Two hearts staying on one level throughout the movement will stay together much more easily.
The front leg moves back with the torso.	The front leg is never left extended in front of the dancer's body, as it would interfere with the partner's movement and, more importantly, the leg would be decoupled from the dancer's own heart, requiring muscular effort on the dancer's part to bring it back to the standing position. Training the leg to move with the torso also facilitates the correct step forwards.
The back leg folds as the torso moves back, allowing the torso to stay constantly at the same level.	If the back leg remained straight as the torso moved back then the torso would be forced up, lifting the heart away from the partner's heart, and tearing apart the relationship between the two hearts. Instead, a loose, soft leg passively bends as the torso moves smoothly back.
The heart, the front leg and the back heel arrive in the final standing position all at the same time.	A common mistake is to drop the heel of the back foot as the transfer begins. This has the effect of straightening the leg, which compromises the connection of the hearts through the transfer of the heart backwards. The entire body moves together, because of its connection to the heart. Nothing arrives separately.

The follower keeps the intention of the heart moving forwards towards the leader's heart, even though the leader is carrying the follower's heart backwards	The follower's intention forwards allows the follower to maintain the presence that the leader requires for the connection between the two hearts. If the follower takes her or his own heart back instead of making the leader carry it back, the follower's heart will inevitably move away from the leader's heart, creating a shunting action rather than the smooth, unified motion of two hearts together. This would give the leader the sense of the follower constantly running away from the leader – the sense of trying to catch hold of smoke. The hearts would not feel connected.
When the leader steps back, the leader carries the follower's heart forwards.	If the leader pulled the heart away when stepping back, the relationship between the hearts would be broken. The leader's intention is forwards towards the follower's heart even while taking both bodies back.

Stepping Forwards for the Leader

Stepping forwards correctly is the secret of good leading. The leader's step forwards is a movement of the heart, directly towards and then through the follower's heart. The leader aims always towards the very centre of the follower.

Technical skill	How this skill keeps the two hearts together
The leader's step forwards begins with the movement of the leader's heart through the follower's heart.	As the leader's heart moves through the follower's heart, it first leads the extension of the leg; then carries the follower's torso back. If the leader did not move through the follower's heart, the follower's body would be unable to feel with the same precision and subtlety the lead for the extension, and the follower would not be able to allow the heart to be carried to the end of the step correctly. The connection between the hearts would be lost.
As the follower's heart moves back, the leader's heart follows the follower's heart.	For the follower to stay in balance at the end of the step, the follower's heart must end the step directly over the balls of the toes of the follower's supporting foot. If the follower's foot is not exactly where the leader anticipated, and the leader is to keep the two hearts together and keep the two dancers in balance, then the leader's heart must end the movement exactly in front of where the follower's heart actually is, which is to say exactly in front of the follower's supporting foot, wherever that may be. The length of the leader's step will be the same as the length of the follower's step. If the leader tried to carry the hearts to where the leader anticipated that the step would end, the leader would either force the follower out of balance – something which is uncomfortable, potentially even dangerous, and which would jolt the follower out of the ideal meditative state, if the follower had ever reached it – or tear apart the relationship between the two hearts. Leaders in the Golden Age acquired this skill by learning to follow, and then applied it to their leading, following the follower though each step.

The leader's foot hangs from the leader's heart, and arrives at the last possible moment.	If the leader moved the foot first, and placed it where the leader anticipated the step would end, but the follower ended the step somewhere else, again the leader would either tear apart the relationship between the two hearts or force one of the dancers to be out of balance. By allowing the foot to land under the leader's heart, and the leader's heart to travel with the follower's heart, the leader will place the foot exactly where it needs to be to keep the two hearts in front of each other and the two dancers comfortably in balance, and the leader's step will be exactly the same length as the follower's step.
Once the step is completed, the leader allows the back foot to fall back into the standing position.	The leader uses no muscular effort to bring the two legs together, but allows the free leg to fall back into the standing position under the action of gravity.

Stepping Forwards for the Follower

The follower's step forwards, like the leader's, begins in the heart. The follower does not extend the foot forwards. Instead, the foot hangs from the follower's heart, and goes where the leader takes it. The foot, like the heart, is searching for the centre of the leader's body.

Technical skill	How this skill keeps the two hearts together
The follower's heart follows the leader's heart through the movement.	As for the leader, when moving forwards the follower must allow the heart to move, and allow the foot to arrive last. There is no extension for the follower when stepping forwards. (Some Golden Age styles used a longer step, requiring what might have looked like a slight extension forwards on the part of leader and follower, but the foot still arrived under the heart at the end of the step.)
The follower's foot lands directly underneath the follower's heart on the music.	Once again, the music, as the third member of the couple, helps the leader to know when the follower has completed this part of the step, thus allowing the leader to start leading the next movement.
The follower allows the back leg to fall into the standing position.	The follower uses no muscular effort to hold the two legs together. This would interfere with the next movement the leader leads, as it would break the connection between the leg and the heart.

Stepping to the Side

To make sure the hearts are together at the end of a step to the side, the leader leads a side step in the same way that the leader leads the follower to step back: the leader initiates the movement of the follower's heart, the follower extends the foot to the side in the direction of the movement of the hearts, and the leader follows the follower's heart through the transfer of weight, so that they remain together throughout.

A side step functions in the same way as a step forwards for the leader and back for the follower. The movement of the leader's heart leads the follower's extension, the leader transfers the follower's weight, and the leader's feet arrive last. This ensures that at the end of the side step the hearts remain together.

Technical skill	How this skill keeps the two hearts together
A step to the side for the follower is like a step back, and for the leader is like a step forwards.	The follower's side step begins with an extension along the line of the hips, which is the line of the shoulders. The leader initiates it by carrying the follower's heart to the side. The leader then follows the follower through the side step. The leader's foot arrives at the end of the follower's step, ensuring the two hearts are kept together, in the same way as when the follower steps back and the leader steps forwards.

Transferring the Follower's Weight from One Foot to the Other in the Standing Position

Although this would appear to be one of the simplest moves possible, it in fact requires precision on the part of both dancers if it is to be done correctly. If the follower stands with the feet apart, or holds the free foot off the floor, as beginners often do, a movement of the heart that should be large enough to move the follower's heart from one foot to the other will produce no result. And if the leader is not directly in front of the follower, the follower will not feel the lead – the follower may feel nothing at all.

So even though this move seems quite simple, it is something of a test of skill on both parts for the leader to lead a change of foot when the follower may not be expecting it.

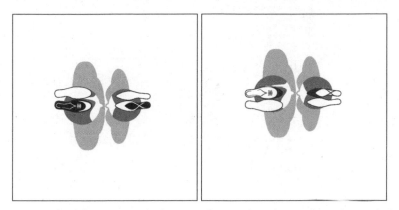

Moving the follower's weight from one foot to the other involves moving the follower's heart a distance approximately equal to the width of a foot.

Technical skill	How this skill keeps the two hearts together
The leader carries the follower's heart from directly over one foot to directly over the other.	Both dancers are standing on one leg, with the free leg hanging passively at its side. The movement of the leader's heart from directly over the balls of the toes of one foot to directly over the balls of the toes of the other foot is enough to lead the transfer of the follower's weight if both dancers are in the correct position.
The follower always stands with the weight all on one leg, with the other leg hanging passively at its side.	If the follower uses no muscular effort then the free leg will fall next to the supporting leg. The movement of the heart required to move the weight from one foot to the other is tiny – no more than the width of a foot. If the follower uses muscular effort to keep weight off the free foot then it is almost impossible for the leader to lead the follower to put weight on it. If the follower stands with the feet apart, then the movement of the heart necessary to carry it from one foot to the other would be much larger. The movement of the leader's heart from one foot to the other could not be felt.
The hearts are directly in front of each other.	If the hearts are slightly displaced, as in the position commonly used for the Ballroom dances, the displacement of the hearts is greater than the distance the heart moves to create the change of weight, making it much harder to feel.

The leader stands with the free leg next to the supporting leg.	If the leader's feet are further apart, the movement of the leader's heart travelling from one foot to the other is large enough to generate a side step for the follower rather than a change of weight. If the leader's feet are together the movement does not lead an extension, simply the change of weight.
The leader can lead the follower to change feet without the leader changing feet.	The small displacement of the two hearts to the side leads the follower to change weight from one foot to the other. The highly skilled leader can move the follower's heart the correct amount without changing the leader's own weight if the leader wishes to do so. It is the movement of the hearts that generates the follower's movement – the leader's feet have nothing to do with it

The Hold

The hold is the basis of Tango. Without the hold, Tango as we know it would not exist.

It is different from the hold used in other couple dances. Most specifically it is different from the hold used in the Ballroom dances, and people with Ballroom experience should take note that breaking the old habit and acquiring the new one takes some concentration and practice.

I was once teaching an older Ballroom dancer, and found I had to keep reminding him that he should be dancing with the woman in front of him, not the woman next to her. He laughed, and said that many years earlier when he started learning Ballroom, his teacher had kept saying to him, 'Don't dance with the woman in front of you – dance with the woman next to her!'

It is a great challenge for a leader coming from a Ballroom background to keep the right shoulder back, and to maintain a right angle between the line of the shoulders and the right upper arm. It may help to remember that in Tango it is never necessary to touch the follower's back with the right hand, and it is often better not to. The lead in Tango does not come from the leader's arms. It comes from the leader's heart. Any pressure at all on the follower's back tends to be uncomfortable, and may even compromise the follower's balance, as the balance has already been taken as far forwards as it is possible for it to be. In Ballroom the follower's balance is further back, making the presence of the leader's arm reassuring, but for a skilled follower this is not the case in Tango. The follower needs the leader's heart to come forwards towards her or him, so that the leader is making the offer of coming together, and the follower can then choose whether to accept it. The leader who pulls the follower forwards with his or her right arm (often without realising), makes the skilled follower uncomfortable, and compromises the follower's balance. Leaders who learned to dance in the prácticas often danced with no contact at all between their right arm or hand and the follower's back.

If the leader tried to make contact between the right hand and the follower's back, this would often pull the leader's right shoulder forward, twisting the leader's upper body, and pulling the leader's heart away from the follower. Followers in the Golden Age chose contact with the leader's heart over contact with the leader's hand.

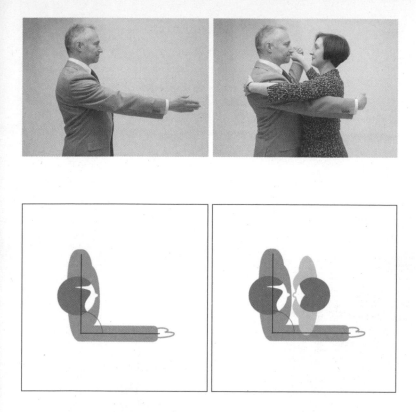

The leader's right arm extends directly forwards so that the line of the leader's upper arm makes a 90-degree angle with the line of the leader's shoulders when viewed from above. (The leader's hand may be lower than the leader's shoulder to allow the leader's arm to fit under the follower's shoulder. If the follower is taller than the leader, the leader's arm will be horizontal.) This keeps the follower directly in front of the leader at all times. The leader does not attempt to put the hand on the follower's back as this would pull the leader's shoulder forwards. The extent to which the arm bends around the follower will depend on how the two bodies fit together and how close the couple chooses to dance.

In the south of Buenos Aires it was common for a follower to look forwards and past the leader's right ear. In the north of the city it was far more common for a woman to look to her own right. This was for social, rather than technical, reasons. Looking straight forward, which brought the follower's mouth close to the leader's ear, and vice versa, meant that things could be whispered during the dance. Nice girls didn't do that sort of thing, so in the more respectable parts of town a less potentially compromising position was adopted.

Also, a follower did not place the left hand on the back of the leader's neck. This was seen as a statement of possession, and a warning to other followers not to dance with that particular leader. In the younger generation, unaware of that significance, it has become quite common.

Even if the follower was looking forwards, the dancers did not look into each other's eyes. In a close hold they were too close together for it to be pleasant, and at any distance having someone stare at you can be disconcerting. Besides, the leader had the vital duty of keeping a lookout in order to be able to prevent collisions. The leader focused on the follower with the heart. The eyes needed to be alert to the situation in the room.

For that reason, too, whether the follower looked forwards or to the right, the follower did not push the head against the leader's head, as that would block the leader's field of vision.

Technical skill	How this skill keeps the two hearts together
The two dancers stand directly in front of each other with the shoulders parallel.	This places the two hearts together at the start of the dance, and keeps them together throughout any and all movements. Golden Age dancers referred to this as maintaining the relationship between the two bodies – *manteniendo la relación entre los dos cuerpos.*

The leader's right arm extends directly forwards, so that there is a right angle at the leader's right shoulder when viewed from above.	The leader's right upper arm is kept on a line parallel to the line joining the two hearts. This prevents the follower from slipping to the side, away from the leader's heart.
The leader does not attempt to touch the follower's back with his or her right hand.	This often surprises people, who expect an embrace in which the leader's right arm is used to lead the follower. However, in Tango the lead does not come from the leader's arm, but from the leader's heart. If the leader tries to place the right hand on the follower's back there are several negative consequences.
	The follower is in a finely balanced state. Anything that impinges on the follower's balance becomes uncomfortable and distressing. And pressure from the leader on the follower's back interferes with the follower's balance. This would not be a problem if the follower's body leaned back, away from the leader, as it does in the competitive Ballroom dances. In that case the leader's hand on the follower's back might be pleasant, even useful. However, in Tango the follower has the weight at the extreme forward balance point, on the balls of the toes. Any additional pressure forwards causes problems and discomfort for the follower who dances with Golden Age technique.
	Also, in trying to get the right hand onto the follower's back, the leader will in most cases end up pulling the right shoulder forwards, out of alignment. This twists the leader's torso, pulling the heart away from the follower, tending to shift the

	follower over to the leader's right, into a position more like that used by Ballroom dancers. This was not the position used in Buenos Aires in the Golden Age.

My experience dancing with leaders who learned in the Golden Age was that they practically never touched my back with their right arm or hand. They brought their heart towards me, and allowed me to decide how closely I danced with them. They only ever used their right arm if dancing with an inexperienced follower who did not know how to follow them and needed extra support, and even then the arm was generally used only as a crash barrier to prevent the follower from getting away if the follower went in the wrong direction. If the follower crashes into the leader's arm, that does not hurt the follower, whereas the leader using the right arm to control the follower can be uncomfortable or even painful. |
| The follower places the left hand on the leader's back. | The follower stands with the weight at the extreme forward balance point. If the follower placed the hand on the leader's shoulder the hand would become heavy and uncomfortable for the leader. (In the Ballroom dances the follower's weight is back, so the shoulder is the best place for the hand to be.) Placing the hand on the leader's back allows the follower an extra sense of the movement of the leader's heart without becoming a burden on the leader.

Some show dancers choose to place the left hand on the front of the leader's arm, claiming that it improves the follower's balance in complicated moves. The dancers of the Golden |

	Age were able to do those same complicated moves without needing to support themselves in that way. The left hand on the front of the leader's right arm gives the leader the sense of being pushed away, making the dance less pleasant.
The leader's left arm is in line with the leader's shoulders, with the palm of the hand turned in.	Again, because the weight is forwards rather than back, if the leader had the palm facing forwards as is normal in the Ballroom dances, this could cause discomfort for the follower, as the leader's arm would tend to bear down on the follower. By keeping the palm turned in, the leader ensures that there is no downward pressure on the follower's hand.
The follower's right hand in placed in the leader's left, with the palms of the hands touching.	The contact between the palms of the hands is very important, not as a way of keeping the unity of the hearts, but as a reflection of it. The intimacy of the palm-to-palm contact is part of the intimacy created within the Tango couple. Some Golden Age men would place a folded handkerchief between the palms if their hands tended to get sweaty while dancing. But they would never hold any way except palm to palm.
The leader allows the follower to choose the distance between the bodies.	The leader never pulls the follower into the embrace, but brings his or her own heart forwards and allows the follower to set the distance. Throughout the course of the dance the follower maintains a constant distance, thus allowing the hearts to move together whatever the actual distance between them. Pulling the follower in would compromise the follower's balance, and therefore the follower's ability to follow.

Turning

In Tango the follower spends a great deal of the dance turning – not turning around or spinning away from the leader, as in some dances, but changing direction by pivoting. The leader spends a great deal of time pivoting too, but the leader always has the possibility of faking it by doing something different with his or her own feet. The follower does not have that luxury.

It is vital that the follower is able to turn without ever being out of balance. If the follower is out of balance there is a danger that the follower will need to take a step without waiting, in order to avoid falling over. This would destroy the relationship between the two hearts. Some followers get so good at guessing which step the leader is planning to lead next, that when they are out of balance they can take the next step and end up in the right place almost every time. However, even though they ended up in the right place, they did it on their own, and to the dancers of the Golden Age that meant the couple had ceased to exist and the whole meaning of the dance was lost.

So the skills that allow the follower to stay perfectly in balance, with no need to take a step to prevent the follower from falling, are the skills the follower needs to keep the two hearts together. And the follower must be prepared to pivot at all times, as the leader may lead a pivot at any moment.

Naturally, the more perfectly the leader can perform these same skills, the less the leader needs to fake it, and the more control (and the more options) the leader has.

Technical skill	How this skill keeps the two hearts together
The supporting leg is soft and loose.	Although Ballet dancers are taught to turn on a straight leg, the dancer actually has greater stability turning on a leg that is soft and a little bit bent. The soft leg allows for tiny adjustments to compensate for any imperfection in the turn, helping the dancer keep control of the balance at all times.
The weight is on the balls of the toes.	To reduce friction with the floor, the weight should be on the smallest possible area of the shoe. Friction would make turning harder. Ballroom dancers turn either on the toes or the heels. Followers in Tango never turn on their heels, always on the balls of the toes, as the weight is forwards to bring the hearts closer together. Some people recommend that the weight be in the middle of the balls of the toes. Others prefer to think of the ball of the big toe as the end of the leg. The dancer should find what suits their own body. What should be avoided is placing the weight towards the outer edge of the balls of the toes, as a loss of balance while turning in this position could potentially lead to straining the ankle or knee.
The head is balanced on top of the spine.	In order to turn as easily as possible, the centre of the dancer's weight needs to be over the balls of the toes. The head is a very heavy part of the dancer's anatomy. If it comes away from the dancer's vertical axis it can cause a loss of balance.

The free leg hangs from the dancer's heart under the action of gravity.	The leg is also very heavy. If the leg is lifted during a turn, not only does it give an aesthetically unappealing dog-at-a-lamppost look, it also has the potential to pull the dancer off balance. However, the free leg should not be held next to the supporting leg by muscular effort, as this interferes with the follower's ability to follow the next step. The leader might move the follower's heart, but the free leg, resolutely clamped to the supporting leg, would fail to move with the heart, causing the follower to fall into the next step. The leg must be allowed to hang freely from the heart to allow the next step to happen naturally. Gravity itself will keep the leg close to the axis of the pivot, if the dancer allows it to do so.

The Turning Walk – the True Basic of Golden Age Tango

In modern Tango classes around the world, almost universally some form of the salida is taught to beginners as their 'Basic Step'. The dancers who learned in the práctica were freed from the need to find a step that they could learn before they understood the Tango. The understanding came first, and the steps later. If they thought in terms of a basic at all (and not all of them did), to many their basic was the turning walk – the natural turning pattern of the follower's steps when the leader led the follower's heart to move in a curve.

This pattern is not a 'step' in the sense that we would normally understand the word. It is a natural movement, given the constraints of the Tango, which the leader can rely on the follower's body to make.

Imagine the follower is standing on the right leg, and the leader, standing on the spot, turns the follower's heart clockwise. The follower will need to take a step with the left leg, and that step will need to keep the relationship between the two hearts constant. So the follower will take a side step with the left that carries the follower around the leader on the arc of a circle with the leader at its centre.

If that step has been taken and the leader continues to stand on the spot and continues to carry the follower's heart round clockwise the follower will need to take another step. That step must be with the right foot, as it is the right foot that the follower has free. It cannot be a side step. The follower's right leg cannot pass through the follower's left leg, which is solid. It must go either in front of it or behind it. In this example our follower has not yet started the turning walk, so the leader must lead the next step either forwards or back. Let us imagine that to get into the walk the leader leads the follower's next step to be forwards by carrying the follower's heart in front of the follower's left leg. (This will require the leader to change the position of the centre of the circle slightly.)

If the leader now continues to carry the follower's heart clockwise, the follower's next step will again be a side step with the left, carrying the follower's body round the circumference of a circle at the centre of which is the leader's heart.

If the leader continues to carry the follower's heart clockwise, the follower must take a step with the right leg, and this step will be a step back – not because the follower has learned a sequence, but because the natural swing of the follower's hips moving from the forward step to the side step makes the most natural next step for the follower to be a back step. The leader could lead the follower to take another forward step – the leader can lead any physically possible step at any time. To lead the follower to take a forwards step would be to interrupt the natural movement of the follower's body, involving a change of direction. If the leader simply carries the follower's heart around another segment of the circle, the follower's next step will naturally be a back step.

If the leader continues to carry the follower's heart clockwise, the next step must be a side step as before, and if the leader continues to carry the follower's heart clockwise, the next natural step will be a step forwards, again, because of the natural movement of the follower's body as it goes from back step to side step. The leader could change the direction of the follower's motion and lead another back step. But the natural movement for the follower is to take a forwards step.

So the most natural and comfortable movement for the follower to do if the leader is leading the follower to walk around the leader's heart is a cycle of forwards–side–back–side–forwards–side–back–side.

The cycle of the turning walk – forwards, side, back, side, forwards.

Each step is individually led and followed. The follower is not a billiard ball that will continue in motion unless stopped. The leader leads each step by carrying the follower's heart around the next segment of the circle. By leading each step to flow from the last, rather than interrupting that flow, the leader makes the natural movement of the follower's legs fall into that cycle – forwards–side–back–side–forwards.

This movement also relies on the follower taking accurate side steps. If the follower's side step carries the follower away from the leader, then forwards-side-forwards might become the natural movement. If the follower's side step is accurate then the turning walk becomes the natural movement.

The turn created by one cycle of the turning walk will vary from couple to couple and from moment to moment. It is extremely unlikely that one cycle will make a complete circle. As a rule of thumb, roughly six steps are usually needed to make one complete turn. The precise distance turned, though, will depend on many factors.

The leader may lead the follower into the cycle at any step, starting with a side step, a forwards step or a back step. The leader may stop the cycle at any step. The leader may also reverse the direction of the turn at any step, going from a forwards step in one direction to a forwards step in the other (forwards ocho), from a back step to a back step (backwards ocho) or from a side step to a side step.

The dancers of the Golden Age understood the patterns they led in terms of how they combined straight steps and turning walk steps. Because they had a thorough grasp of this grammar of Tango, they understood how and when the follower moved from one kind of walk to the other, rather than learning each example as a figure. This gave them tremendous choreographic freedom.

Leading the Turning Walk

A common mistake made by unskilled Tango dancers is to assume that the follower needs a signal to indicate the direction of the turning walk. Inexperienced leaders assume it is easier for the follower to understand if the leader turns ahead of the follower. Nothing could be further from the truth.

The leader must carry the follower's heart through each step of the turning walk, just as the leader carries the follower's heart through every other step in the Tango. The two hearts must stay together all the time.

Throughout the turning walk the hearts remain together.

The sensation is that the two hearts travel in smooth concentric curves. If the leader stands on the spot, the follower's heart moves on a circle around the leader's heart. The leader may change the shape of the curve by moving his or her own heart – which is the centre of the follower's circle – making the two hearts twin stars in orbit around each other. The line joining the two hearts is never distorted. The shoulders stay parallel and in front of each other throughout the turn, as they are at all times.

The Forwards Step for the Follower while Turning

When the follower takes a step forwards, the follower's heart is moved by the leader's heart, with the follower's free leg hanging passively under the follower's heart. The follower's free leg falls directly underneath the follower's heart wherever the leader has placed it on the beat of the music. The follower's foot is on the line that joins the two hearts, which is also a line perpendicular to the follower's hips, which are directly under the follower's shoulders.

The shape that is traced by the follower's heart, and therefore the follower's foot hanging from it, is controlled by the movement of the leader's heart. If the leader is stepping straight back then the follower's heart and the follower's foot travel straight forwards along the line joining the two hearts. If the leader leads the follower to step forwards by turning rather than by stepping back then the shape traced by the follower's heart and therefore the follower's foot is a curve. The follower's heart and foot travel straight forwards on the line that joins the two hearts, but the leader changes the position of that line through the course of the step.

How well the follower performs the turning forwards step has a huge impact on how pleasant that follower is to dance with. It is common to see inexperienced followers stepping away from their leader when taking the forwards step. This is an understandable mistake for the follower to make. The follower will have been told that a step forwards must go straight forwards, perpendicular to the line of the follower's hips. This is perfectly accurate. However, if the follower took that step straight out along the line perpendicular to the position of the follower's hips at the beginning of the step, rather than waiting for the foot, the heart and the hips to be led to the final position, the result would generally be that the follower would end up stepping away from the leader.

This action would tear apart the relationship between the two hearts.

At the end of the step the follower would either have the heart over the foot, pulling the heart away from the leader, or be out of balance, causing the follower to fall into the next step without waiting for the leader to carry the heart, which would also pull the heart away from the leader. To dancers who learned in the Golden Age this would have been a violation of the purpose of Tango technique, which was to bring the two hearts together.

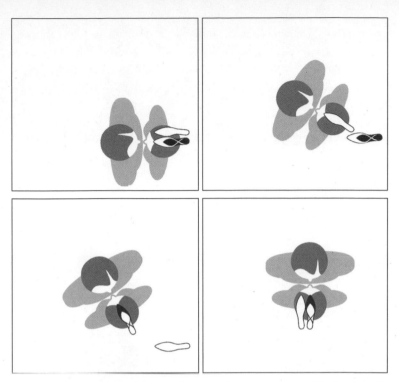

A turning forwards step happens because the leader turns while leading the follower to take a step forwards. The degree of turn depends on how the step is led and how the two bodies move together.

The amount of turn and the direction taken are led by the leader. At different times a turning forwards step may have different lengths and may carry the follower in different directions. However, the one constant is that the follower is always carried into the leader's heart.

The Forwards Ocho

Modern Tango dancers are often taught exercises for the forwards ocho that may lead them to assume that a well-performed ocho is a zigzag combination of straight lines in one direction and then another. This was not how Golden Age dancers danced the forwards ocho. To them it was a combination of curves. The follower traces a curve first clockwise directly into the leader's heart and then anticlockwise directly into the leader's heart.

The leader's heart, of course, travels with the follower's heart, turning clockwise to lead the clockwise step and anticlockwise to lead the anticlockwise step. The follower's heart is moving towards the leader's heart throughout the step. The leader's heart is turned to point directly at the follower's heart throughout the step, as it must be at all times.

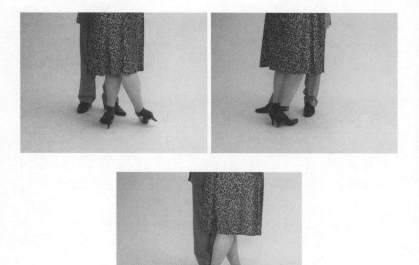

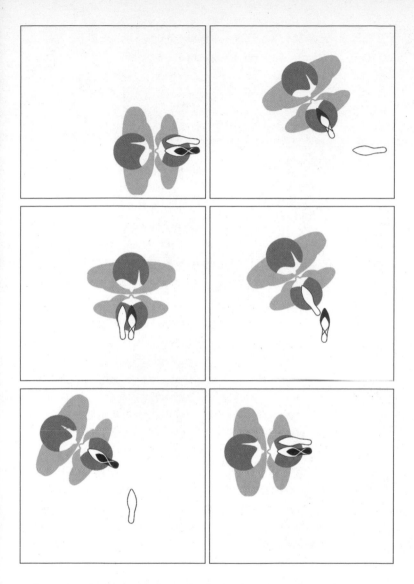

A forwards ocho happens when a leader leads a turning forwards step in one direction followed by a turning forwards step in the opposite direction.

It is important for the leader to remember when leading the follower through a forwards ocho that the follower's supporting leg is solid and the follower's other leg cannot move through it. When changing the follower's direction from a turning step in one direction to a turning step in the other direction the leader must lead the follower's moving leg around the supporting leg. The leader must make sure the hearts are together, so that at the end of the follower's first turning step the follower's heart is indeed directly over the follower's foot. The leader can then easily turn the follower in the opposite direction.

The leader follows the follower through the movement, in the same way that the leader follows the follower through a step back. The leader must never turn away from the follower when leading a forwards ocho, or any other turning step. The leader turns with the follower, preserving the unity of the hearts throughout the step – and therefore the leader's control.

The Cross

As danced by the dancers of the Golden Age, the cross was also a turning forwards step for the follower – albeit one that actually travelled in a backwards direction.

In the salida, the cross is the follower's fourth step. The follower has taken a side step with the right, followed by a back step with the left. The leader then leads the extension of a straight walking step with the follower's right leg. Instead of leading the transfer straight back to complete the straight walking step, the leader turns the follower's heart during the transfer. The follower's left leg hangs from the follower's heart, and as the leader changes the direction of movement of the follower's heart, the leg travels with it. While the leader carries the follower's heart back the leader also carries it round in an anticlockwise direction. The resulting line drawn by the movement is the shape of a reversed letter 'J'.

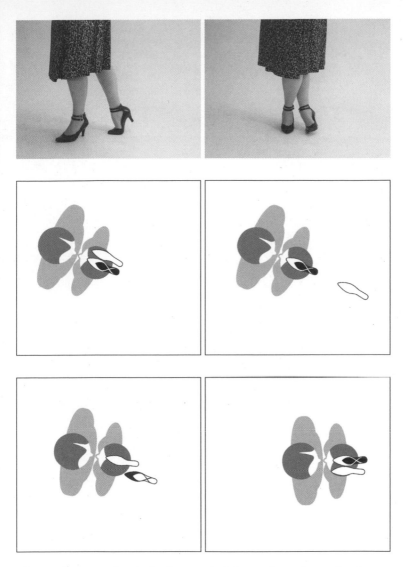

The cross happens when the leader turns the follower during the transfer of a step back with the follower's right foot. If the turn happened too late, after the transfer had been completed, the leader would find he or she had led the extension of a turning back step instead.

The width and depth of the cross are led and followed. There is no one 'correct' way to do the cross – the correct cross is the one that keeps the hearts together. The leader must remember, though, that there are physical limits to how wide or deep the follower's cross can be. The leader must be sensitive and, as always, follow the follower through the movement to ensure the hearts stay together.

It is only possible to lead and follow the cross in the way in which the dancers of the Golden Age did it if the follower walks backwards correctly.

Technical skill	How this skill allows the cross to be led and followed
The follower extends the foot straight back on the line joining the two hearts.	If the follower walks backwards placing the feet on two parallel lines it is much harder for the follower to feel the lead for the cross. The turn required to get the follower's left foot across the follower's right will be much greater if the follower's right foot is further to the right than the leader expected it to be, so the leader will have to lead a larger turn from the outset. Otherwise the follower's feet may end up side by side, and not in the cross. But if the placement of the follower's right foot is unpredictable, it will be hard for the leader to feel how large a turn is necessary to get the follower into the cross this time, and the consequence might be that the cross does not happen.
The follower allows the free left leg to hang passively from the heart and go wherever the leader takes the heart.	If the follower pulls the left leg in, having been trained to 'bring the legs together', the follower is forced to guess whether the leader is going to lead the cross or not. The result of this is that often followers do the cross without being led because they think the leader is leading a

	salida, denying the leader the opportunity to lead any other variation at that point. Also, the leader is denied the possibility of going into the cross from straight walking, as the follower pulls the foot in beside the other before the turn can be led.
	At the other extreme, if the follower takes the body back while leaving the left leg extended in front – a very common mistake made by people new to Tango – then the leader has no way of indicating to the follower where the foot is to go, as the follower has disconnected the foot from the heart. A skilled leader may be able to move the follower's heart sufficiently to persuade the follower to take the foot across. A beginner would find this hard.
The follower does not 'do' the cross, but allows the cross to happen.	A follower who placed the foot into the cross her or himself would be destroying the relationship between the two hearts. The follower must allow the left leg to hang from the heart, and allow the leader to carry it where it needs to be, whether or not that is the cross.

Leading and following the cross in the way in which it was done by dancers from the Golden Age involves a high level of technical skill. A skilled leader can reasonably easily lead an unskilled follower, once the leader has got to know the follower's particular technical flaws. For two unskilled dancers dancing together the cross presents something of a challenge. However, in the Tango Renaissance the experience of the majority of dancers is that it is one of the first things they are taught. This has led to some confusion.

Some dancers as beginners were told that the cross should be done automatically in the salida without a lead. When this was said for the first time by someone trying to teach Tango to a new dancer, they probably meant it just as a stopgap solution, until the dancer learned to walk properly. Whatever the reason, though, as time went by, people who were told that as beginners went on to dance with or teach other beginners, and a new way of dancing emerged in the Tango Renaissance that relied on the follower doing the cross without being led.

Other dancers developed their own ways of leading the follower into the cross, and there are now many different versions in use around the world – even in Buenos Aires.

Of all the ingenious ways people have found of solving the problem of the cross, the method used in the Golden Age still seems to me to be the most seductive, the softest, the warmest and the most intimate. In the eyes of the Golden Age dancers, that would make it the best.

The Back Step for the Follower while Turning

The inexperienced follower is often told that it is necessary to learn to dissociate the hips from the shoulders, so that the shoulders may turn one way while the hips turn the other, with the shoulders and the hips staying horizontal. The reason this is important is for the back step in the turning walk.

If the follower steps forwards correctly then it is not necessary to dissociate when doing a forwards ocho or the forwards step of the turning walk. If the follower steps forwards imperfectly, then dissociation helps keep the two hearts together, and for that reason it is taught, but the follower dancing with Golden Age technique should have no need to dissociate on any forwards step.

The back step of the turning walk, however, does require dissociation. It is necessary for the follower to extend straight back on a line perpendicular to the hips, placing the foot on the circumference of a circle that passes through the follower's supporting foot and had the leader at its centre. At the same time the follower must keep the heart pointed directly at the leader's heart, as it must be at all times. The leader is leading the extension in the same way the leader would if leading a side step, but the follower is doing it with the other foot.

This requires a tremendous turn of the hips for the follower, and a great deal of torsion in the follower's body. It is one of the hardest things the follower is expected to do on the dance floor.

The Timing of the Turning Walk

The follower's extension in the back step of the turning walk is very hard to do correctly. The transfer of the back step and the side step that comes after it release the tension set up by the twist in the follower's body and absorb the momentum generated by the large turn of the hips. If the turning walk is allowed to flow naturally, then the side step that follows the back step will arrive on the half beat of the music, with the forwards step arriving on the next beat.

This is not because the follower has learned the rhythm as the correct way of performing a routine. It is the natural consequence of good technique used to carry out this movement. The walk itself naturally springs from correct Golden Age Tango technique applied to the follower walking in a circle round the leader. The rhythm also springs naturally from the technique used by Golden Age dancers.

One cycle of the turning walk, which is four steps for the follower, naturally takes three beats of the music.

Forwards		Side		Back	Side	Forwards
1		2		3	and	1

The difficult extension of the back step sets up a tension that the relatively easy movements that follow it release.

The Backwards Ocho

When a back step is led in the turning walk, the flow of the movement leads the follower to dissociate the hips from the shoulders, allowing the extension of the follower's foot into the back step to travel along the line of the follower's shoulders. If a back step that is turned by the leader does not come out of the turning walk, then that is not the case.

A backwards ocho is a turning back step in one direction followed by a turning back step in the other direction. As it does not come out of the flow of the turning walk, the follower will not dissociate the hips from the shoulders, and the leader must carry the follower through the motion in the normal way.

The leader leads the extension by moving through the follower's heart along the line joining the hearts, and then follows the follower's heart as it travels back to its position directly over the back foot. While following the follower's heart, the leader also turns it, so that when the step is complete, the direction of the line joining the two hearts has changed.

To be comfortable for the follower, a backwards ocho must travel. The follower walks backwards in a zigzag and the leader travels with the follower.

A backwards ocho is a turning back step in one direction followed by a turning back step in the opposite direction.

What Is the Leader Doing with His or Her Own Feet During Turning Steps?

The simplest answer to this question is: anything that does not interfere with the leader's ability to keep the two hearts perfectly together.

Naturally, some variations are more aesthetically pleasing than others. Some variations need greater levels of skill to perform them without destroying the relationship between the hearts. Some variations suit one leader's body but not another.

The Golden Age dancers produced a huge repertoire of variations, and constantly experimented in the práctica in the search for new and better ones. Starting to learn the variations they used is like opening a box of chocolates – so many lovely things to choose from!

In essence, though, what the leader does with his or her feet while leading the follower to turn is make sure the leader's heart can carry the follower's heart to where it needs to go without the leader falling over. At its simplest this could mean a slight shuffle to get the feet into the right place, or no movement of the feet at all.

Advanced Techniques

It would be possible to dance for a lifetime exploring the possibilities of the straight and turning walks, and one would never fully exhaust them all. Nevertheless, anyone interested in Tango is sure to be interested in exploring the kicks and flicks that are such a spectacular and flamboyant part of the dance, and that are frequently seen in Tango stage performances.

Modern Tango dancers are sometimes surprised to find that the social dancers in Buenos Aires in the Golden Age danced these same kicks and flicks on the social dance floor. They find it hard to believe these advanced moves are not some new form of Tango created by the new generation of dancers. Indeed, some go as far as to call these moves 'Tango Nuevo' – new Tango. Of course, all living things change, and there will be new things in Tango. So far, though, I myself have yet to see a dancer claiming to do 'Tango Nuevo' doing any move I have not already seen done by someone who learned to dance in the Golden Age. Some people may genuinely believe they have come up with something new, and may never have seen a Golden Age dancer doing that move, even if the move was in fact common in the Golden Age. And it is quite possible there have been some innovations that I simply have never encountered. If that has not already happened then it is sure to happen in the future.

Sacadas

The word 'sacada' comes from the verb *sacar* – to take out or remove. It describes a class of steps where the optical illusion is that the leader knocks the follower's leg out of place.

A Golden Age dancer would never actually displace the follower's leg by knocking it away. To do that would be far too dangerous. If the follower had any weight on a leg and the leader knocked or kicked it then there would be a real risk of injury to the knee or ankle. And if the leader knocked the follower shin to shin or knee to knee, the bony parts of the leg hitting each other could cause pain and bruising – much more pain to the follower, as the one being hit, than to the leader as the one doing the hitting.

Obviously, to the Golden Age dancers that would be completely unacceptable.

A sacada happens usually in a follower's side step, sometimes in a follower's back step, during the transfer. The leader extends the leg forwards, violating the rule of never having the foot in front of the heart. The leader extends the foot along the line joining the two hearts during the transfer, while the follower's legs are apart. The leader aims directly for the follower's heart with both the leader's heart and leg. The leader's heart travels directly through the follower's heart. The extra force generated gives extra momentum to the follower's step, which in turn leads the follower's free leg to swing (or if the movement has been soft, to wrap around the leader's leg before falling away). This is not because the leg has been knocked – it has not – or because the follower lifts it. It is the result of the extra momentum given by the leader's more powerful movement through the follower's body.

If there is any actual contact between the leader's leg and the follower's leg it happens right at the top of the thigh – the fleshiest part of the leg – allowing the contact to be soft, and not painful to the follower.

The extra force of the leader's movement through the follower's heart lifts the follower's free leg from the floor.

The Back Sacada

While a conventional sacada violates a rule by requiring the leader to extend the foot in front of the leader's own heart (and actually behind the follower's heart), the back sacada violates the most fundamental rule in Tango — maintaining the relationship between the two hearts.

A back sacada functions in the same way as a conventional sacada. The leader extends a leg through and behind the follower's heart during the transfer in (generally) a back step for the follower. The difference is that the leader steps back.

In order to do this the leader must break the relationship and turn his or her back on the follower. The leader places his or her hips parallel to the line joining the follower's feet — that is, parallel to the line that joined the two hearts at the moment the extension was led. The leader extends back directly through the follower's heart. Once the foot is behind the follower's heart the leader transfers weight onto it.

The effect is essentially the same as in a conventional sacada, although it is more spectacular. It is also more dangerous. In my early days as a Tango dancer I lost count of the number of times inexperienced leaders drew blood from my ankles or shins trying to do back sacadas.

If the leader aims directly for the follower's heart, then the danger is lessened. The leader must also keep the foot as close to the floor as possible, and as soft as possible. Jabbing back with the heel in the air increases the risk of catching the follower's leg. Heels are hard and surprisingly sharp. They can cause a follower a great deal of pain.

The leader turns away from the follower in order to step back between the follower's legs. The additional force of the leader's body through the follower's heart lifts the follower's foot from the ground.

Boleos (Voleos)

No one knows whether the name of this movement is 'boleo' – related to the *boleadoras*, the hunting weapon of the gaucho, with its powerful whiplash action – or 'voleo' – from the verb *volar*, to fly. Tango was an oral culture, and in Spanish the consonants 'b' and 'v' are practically interchangeable. Many modern authors favour voleo. I prefer boleo because the whip-crack image seems so closely related to good technique in this movement.

A boleo happens when the leader leads the extension of a turning back step and then reverses the direction, leading the follower to bring the same leg round into a turning forwards step.

If this is done slowly the follower's foot will slide along the floor, producing a soft and sensuous movement. If the movement is done with more speed the follower's foot will be lifted from the floor. This does not happen because the follower lifts the foot. It happens because of the momentum given to the leg by the speed with which the leader changes direction.

Imagine a toy train sitting on a track. If I take hold of the engine and gently start to move it forwards along the track, each carriage will be gently pulled into motion, couple by couple, until the whole train is moving. If I take hold of the engine and suddenly move it forwards at speed, then the final carriage of the train will probably fly into the air and be derailed.

If the follower has perfect posture and perfect technique then the follower's foot can be lifted by the leader in much the same way, and will then naturally fall into the right place at the end of the movement.

The follower should never lift the foot her or himself. The foot is behind the follower. The leader can see if there is a clear space on the dance floor but the follower cannot. It would be both rude and dangerous for the follower to kick the foot in the air, as the foot could easily make contact with another dancer. This can be painful. Quite serious injuries have been known to happen on the dance floor when a follower wearing stiletto heels has kicked another dancer.

A leader with good technique will always try to avoid collisions. There is absolutely no excuse for leading a high boleo when there are other couples anywhere near enough to be kicked. And a follower with good technique will never lift a foot into a space that might be occupied by another dancer that the follower is not in a position to see. The follower must trust the leader to be the judge, and never do a boleo that is not led.

Not only that, but lifting the foot produces a far less aesthetically pleasing movement. It is almost impossible for the follower to re-create intentionally the clean, sharp movement created by a natural and technically correct boleo. By comparison, a follower lifting her or his own leg looks rather insipid.

The boleo begins with the extension of a turning back step, either in a turn, or in a backwards ocho. Instead of leading the transfer of the turning back step, the leader reverses the movement into a turning forwards step. The follower has the heart over the front leg, and the leader turns the follower's heart directly over the follower's foot. This has the effect of winding the back leg in, so that the knee of the back leg is inside the back of the knee of the supporting leg. (The back leg is loose and relaxed, even as it extends.) The leader continues to turn the follower's heart over the front leg, and then leads a turning forwards step with the follower's other leg.

So if the original extension back had been made with the follower's left leg, the leader would then turn the follower's heart, directly over the follower's right foot, in a clockwise direction, until the leader could lead a turning forwards step in the anticlockwise direction with the follower's left leg. The mirror image would happen if the original step had been in the opposite direction.

The faster the change of direction is led, the higher the follower's foot will fly (provided the follower has perfect posture, and allows the free leg to be loose and soft). The softer the follower's leg, the sharper the movement will be, just as the softest whip is supposed to have the sharpest crack. If the follower uses any muscular effort to lift the foot the effect is far less aesthetically pleasing.

The faster the change of direction, though, the greater the danger that the follower is in if the leader does not lead correctly. Most specifically, the leader must never under any circumstances use any pressure from his or her arms on the follower's body while leading this movement. The follower has a great deal of momentum, and is relying on the perfect balance that comes from perfect posture. Any force, no matter how slight, from the leader's arm may be enough to take the follower out of balance, and the result can be strained muscles or turned joints. Friends of mine have been off the dance floor for weeks at a time because a leader led a high boleo incorrectly. When done correctly the movement is safe, but done incorrectly it can be quite dangerous.

The leader interrupts the extension of the follower's turning back step, and reverses the turn sharply enough to make the follower's foot fly. The turn winds the follower's free leg in, so that the knee of the moving leg is inside the knee of the supporting leg. The free leg naturally falls back into the correct place as the leader leads a turning step forwards.

Forwards Boleos

The forwards boleo is rarely seen today, but it is one of the loveliest, most seductive and intimate moves in the Tango repertoire.

While the conventional boleo is an interrupted turning back step, the forwards boleo is an interrupted turning forwards step. This may be a forwards step in a turn, a forwards ocho, or the cross.

The forwards boleo requires a high level of skill on the part of both the follower and the leader. For a skilled leader, finding a follower who can follow a forwards boleo is a tremendous and seductive pleasure, greatly enhancing the sense of unity and intimacy in the couple. For the follower, finding a leader with the subtlety of control and appreciation of the follower's own skill to lead the forwards boleo is a compliment and a delight.

The leader begins by moving the follower's heart into a turning forwards step. When the follower's heart (and therefore free leg) is in front of the supporting leg, but before the arrival of the follower's weight onto the follower's front foot, the leader reverses the turn, winding the follower's free leg around the supporting leg. The speed with which the leader leads the change of direction determines how high up the supporting leg the follower's free leg winds itself. (The free leg is soft and loose throughout.) If the change of direction is led softly the foot will stay near the ground. If the change of direction is more sudden the foot may fly higher than the knee. The follower's free leg will always be wound around the knee of the follower's supporting leg. The follower must never use muscular effort to lift the leg. Particularly, the follower must never lift the knee in the air, as there is some danger of making contact with the leader in an unexpected and unpleasant way.

The leader continues to turn the follower's heart, directly over the follower's supporting leg, so that the follower continues to turn, and ends the movement by leading a turning back step. If the movement began with the leader leading the forwards step of an anticlockwise turn, or the cross, then the follower's left leg is led in front of, and then wound around, the follower's right leg, and the movement is finished by the leader leading the follower a turning back step with the follower's left.

The leader changes the direction of the follower's turn before completing a turning forwards step. The follower's free leg wraps around the supporting leg, and then naturally falls back into the correct position as the leader leads a turning back step.

Ganchos

Gancho means hook. A gancho is any movement where one dancer hooks a leg around a leg of the other dancer. This movement always makes a great impression in any stage choreography.

Typically the leader leads the follower to do a gancho by interrupting the transfer of a turning back step. The leader introduces a soft, bent leg into the space between the follower's legs when the follower has extended the leg. As the leader carries the follower's heart towards the back foot, the follower's free leg, hanging passively from the heart, encounters the barrier of the leader's leg. If the leader's leg has been correctly placed, then the momentum in the follower's body will cause the follower's soft, loose leg to wind around the leader's leg. As with the boleo, the softer and looser the follower's leg, the sharper the whip-crack effect as the follower's leg is led into the movement.

The leader's leg must, however, be in exactly the right position. The follower's knee only bends one way. If the leader's leg is placed at the wrong angle then a correct gancho cannot happen. (The result may well be an unintended sacada instead – or a contortion from a follower who is trying to please by doing a gancho that the leader has actually failed to lead.)

The follower must never under any circumstances lift the leg her or himself. Apart from the fact that it looks far less aesthetically pleasing (again, dogs and lampposts are called to mind), it is also dangerous. If the follower kicks then there is a good chance that the follower will kick the leader, and a stiletto heel against the shin can be agony, and can easily draw blood.

To illustrate how the follower's foot flies into the air, imagine a weight hanging from a string, swinging like a pendulum. If I put a finger against the middle of the string the weight will fly up higher than it otherwise would have done, because of the conservation of angular momentum. The weight then naturally falls again and returns to its normal position.

The same thing happens to the follower's leg when it encounters the barrier of the leader's leg. If the follower has perfect posture then the movement of the entire body comes to a stop when the barrier is met. Only the follower's foot can move, and it does so, wrapping itself around the leader's leg. (If the follower does not have perfect posture the momentum may be lost due to the follower's torso swinging back in a kind of dip – something never seen in the Tango in Buenos Aires.)

As with the boleo, the softer and looser the follower's leg, the sharper and cleaner the movement that results.

In this case the leader has reversed the direction of motion of a turning forwards step, changing it into a turning back step, and has created a barrier round which the follower's leg will fly to create the gancho. The barrier must be created in the right direction, as the follower's knee only bends one way. The looser the follower's leg, the sharper the gancho. The follower's leg then naturally falls under the action of gravity, and the leader leads it into a turning forwards step to finish the movement.

A gancho may also be done by the leader. The leader leads the follower into a position where the follower provides the leader with a barrier. The leader inserts the leg and, as with the follower's gancho, allows a loose, soft leg to encounter that barrier. Kicking the foot in the air produces an ugly, gawky effect and is dangerous. Only if the leg meets the barrier and then wraps itself around it is the effect aesthetically pleasing, and the movement safe.

Paradas

Parada comes from the verb parar — to stop. A parada is most commonly led in a turning back step. To lead it, the leader interrupts the transfer of the follower's weight before it is possible for the follower to be completely in balance on the back foot. Stopping the movement of the follower's heart in this position means that the follower must put some weight onto the front foot, dividing the weight between the feet. The leader is therefore violating the fundamental principle that the follower only has weight on one foot at a time, and in doing so effectively immobilises the follower. The follower does not have a free foot, and so cannot move.

The leader brings the follower out of this position by carrying the follower's heart forwards so that it is over the follower's front foot, freeing the follower's back foot to fall into its normal standing position, and allowing the dance to continue.

The pause created by a parada may be so brief as to be almost imperceptible, or, if the music demands it, the leader may take the opportunity to make a movement that is purely decorative, while the follower waits. The latter option is very common in stage choreographies, as it allows the leader to perform as a soloist for a few beats of the music, absolved of the responsibility of dancing as part of a couple, and to have the audience's full attention — and it is commonly followed by a purely decorative movement for the follower so that she or he may take a turn in the spotlight.

On a crowded dance floor, a long pause should be avoided as it would be anti-social, interrupting the flow of all the dancers around the room – and in the worst case it might be dangerous, leading to collisions and possible injury. The social dancer should also be aware that a long, self-indulgent solo decoration while one's partner stands and waits may be selfish and discourteous, whether performed by the leader or the follower – particularly if it is not inspired by the music. (When I was a beginner and knew no better, I indulged in very long and elaborate decorations when led out of a parada thinking they showed off what a good dancer I was, until a dear friend of mine started to refer to this as the "waiting at a bus stop figure" – parada also means bus stop – and I realised quite how rude and thoughtless I had been.)

One common use of the parada is the sandwich – sandwich – or mordida – bite. Having created the parada, the leader slides one foot along or just above the floor until it reaches the edge of the follower's front foot. The leader then slides the other foot along the floor until it meets the other side of the follower's front foot, so that the follower's foot is sandwiched between the leader's feet. (The leader slides his or her own feet so as to avoid the danger of treading on the follower's foot – particularly great here if the leader were to lift and place his or her own feet.)

Having sandwiched the follower's front foot, the leader then takes one foot away, and (having allowed the follower space to decorate if the music requests it) leads the follower into a turning forwards step. It is vital that the leader turns when taking his or her foot away, in order to allow the follower to step forwards without uncomfortable twisting.

The leader must step round, not straight back, when leaving the sandwich, so as to allow the follower to step forwards comfortably. If the leader were to step straight back, the follower stepping forwards would be forced into an uncomfortable, ungainly position, with the legs twisted and the toes turned in. By stepping round, not back, and leading the follower to take a turning forwards step, the leader avoids this, and also keeps the couple together

(Inexperienced followers often misinterpret the placing of one of the leader's feet close to the follower's front foot in a turning back step as a "signal" that the follower should freeze. This is a bad habit and must be broken. It is the movement of the heart that leads the follower to move, and it is the stillness of the heart that leads the follower to be still. Many advanced figures involve the leader placing a foot close to the follower's front foot in a turning back step, as this is a good position for giving more power to the next part of the turn. If the follower were to freeze because of the placement of the leader's foot, ignoring the movement of the leader's heart, the follower would have stopped following, and would have torn the couple apart, causing the leader to struggle to stay in balance and regain connection. The follower would also have prevented the leader from leading many delightful movements.)

Another use of the parada is to change the direction in which the couple is facing. Having created the parada, the leader walks around the follower, turning the follower on the spot. The leader then leads the follower's heart forwards over what is now the front foot (the foot which was the back foot when the parada was created), and the dance can continue.

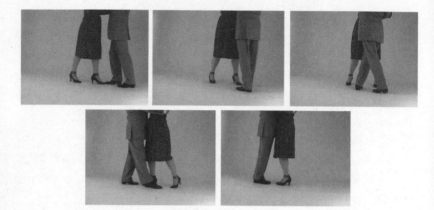

Arrastres

Arrastrar means to drag or sweep along. An arrastre is a step where the leader moves the follower's foot physically, rather than moving it indirectly by moving the follower's heart.

An arrastre is most frequently led in a back step.

The leader leads the extension of the follower's back step. The leader gently slides a foot along the floor until it meets the follower's front foot, and then a little further so that the front of the leader's ankle meets the front of the follower's ankle. The leader begins the transfer of the follower's weight so that the follower's front foot is free. (This is vital – it would be dangerous for the leader to try to move the follower's front foot if there were any weight on it.) The leader uses his or her own foot to carry the follower's free foot, through what is practically the normal standing position (the leader's foot is between the follower's feet, preventing them from brushing, as they normally would), and then to the extension of another step back. The momentum of the movement is such that it is normally most comfortable to complete the second step back. (Turning the second step to lead the cross is also possible if it was the follower's right foot that was carried through the arrastre.)

By carrying the follower's foot with his or her own foot, the leader breaks the relationship between the foot and the heart. The follower continues to allow the free leg to be soft and relaxed, but, instead of gravity carrying the foot under the follower's heart until it is next to the weight-bearing foot (the normal connection between the heart and foot), in this case, because the leader has broken that relationship, gravity makes the follower's foot fall against the leader's foot, allowing it to be moved by the leader's foot. The follower need do nothing. The movement is created by the leader.

The follower must be careful to keep the leg soft and relaxed. If the follower were to stiffen the leg, it would not be possible for the leader to carry the foot through the correct movement.

The leader must NEVER kick the follower, or fling the follower's foot away to move it. The use of any force in this movement is potentially dangerous. I have seen follower's feet covered in bruises because a leader kicked them while trying to lead this movement. And if the leader were to use sufficient force to succeed in moving the follower's foot while it still had weight on it, there would be a risk of injury, as the follower's joints would be under considerable strain.

The leader should also take care to carry the movement through the follower's axis by taking the foot as close as possible to the follower's weight bearing foot. Carrying the follower's foot away from the weight bearing foot would run the risk of taking the follower off balance.

This movement will be most powerful and effective if the inner edge of the leader's foot is against the inner edge of the follower's foot – in other words, if the leader carries the follower's left foot with the leader's left, or the follower's right foot with the leader's right.

Also, for maximum effect, the leader should make sure that the leader's hips are pointing in the direction in which the movement will travel. If the movement is led in a turning back step, this will involve the leader twisting the torso, so that the leader's heart points directly at the follower's heart, while the leader's hips face in the direction of the movement. Because the leader's leg moves along the line perpendicular to the line of the leader's hips, the movement has more power, and also has a much more attractive look.

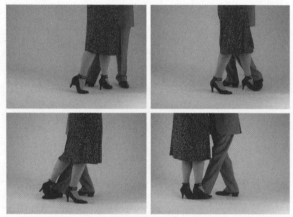

The leader must not push or kick the follower's foot – if the follower still had weight on – the foot any force used by the leader could be painful, or even dangerous

An arrastre in a side step is also possible. In this case the leader inserts a foot (with no weight on it) between the follower's feet during the transfer of a side step. The leader then returns the follower's free foot to its starting position, reversing the side step. Again, the momentum of the movement means that it is normally most comfortable to complete the side step created by the arrastre.

Much rarer, and much more complex, is an arrastre in a turning forwards step. This arrastre demands great care and attention, and above all accuracy, on the leader's part. The movement must be very small or the there is a danger of the follower being pulled off balance. The hearts must stay together throughout. As always, the arrastre can only be done when there is no weight on the foot, and it carries the follower's foot essentially through a normal step.

It is also possible for the leader to lead the follower to sweep the leader's foot.

The leader leads the extension of a turning back step. The leader then slides a foot next to the outer edge of the follower's front foot, placing no weight on it. The leader leads the transfer of the follower's heart, and then the extension of a side step (the next step in the turning walk sequence). The leader allows his or her own leg to be soft and relaxed, allowing gravity to hold it next to the follower's foot as the follower's foot goes through the movement. By carrying the follower's heart, the leader is using the connection between the follower's heart and the follower's foot to move his or her own foot directly.

The follower does not push the leader's foot. The leader leads the follower into the extension of a side step, carrying the follower's heart through the movement to be made by the feet. Followers should remember that the position of the leader's feet should have no impact on what the follower does. The follower's heart always follows the leaders heart, and never the leader's feet.

Leaders should be aware that this movement may make inexperienced followers nervous, as they might feel they are supposed to "do" something. In fact the movement is led by the leader, and the follower simply allows it to happen.

Taking the follower off axis

It is possible for the leader to break the natural connection between the follower's heart and foot. This is done by taking the follower's heart onto the leader's torso, so that the leader is supporting it and physically preventing it from falling.

If the follower is supported by the leader's torso, and the follower feels completely safe, the leader may then carry the follower's heart further forwards, without the follower's foot landing to prevent the follower from falling.

In order for this to work and be comfortable for the follower, the leader must earn the follower's trust, both by respecting the follower's balance throughout the dance up to this point, and, during the movement itself, making sure that the follower feels completely safe and supported at all times.

The couple begins in a close hold position. (If they have been dancing in an open hold up to this point, the leader needs to bring his or her torso towards the follower's torso, while being careful not to invade the space the follower occupies – which itself would take the follower off balance and lead a step. The easiest way to achieve this is in a side step.)

The leader lifts his or her torso, allowing the follower's torso to rest upon it. The follower must have the sense of being carried safely on the leader's body. The leader may then gently back away from the follower, often in a series of very small steps that turn the couple, but always with the sense of lifting the follower's heart, so that the follower can feel safe, and can relax into the movement.

If the leader chooses to turn the movement, it is vital that the leader does not invade the follower's space by moving towards the follower's supporting foot, as that would push the follower off balance.

Because of the asymmetry of the hold, if the movement is turned then it is much more comfortable for the follower if the turn is anticlockwise.

The leader must take great care to keep the torso lifted. The slightest slouch or slump on the part of the leader would undermine the support of the follower's torso and push the follower down, which would be uncomfortable and frightening, and would destroy the sense of safety necessary for this movement to work and be pleasing.

The follower may chose to cross the free leg behind the supporting leg at the ankle, as this gives a more elegant line, and also may help the follower stay in balance. The supporting leg should not be made stiff, but must be kept relaxed.

In order to exit from this position, the leader returns the follower to her or his own axis, usually by leading a step back for the follower, forwards for the leader. The leader moves the follower's heart directly towards the follower's supporting foot, leading an extension. The leader must continue to support the follower's torso until the follower's own balance is regained, usually during the transfer of the step back.

(It is possible for the leader to lead the follower back into balance without leading an extension if it is done extremely gently. As in all steps back, the length of the follower's extension is led by the way the leader begins the movement of the hearts. A movement that is sufficiently gentle will not result in an extension – though the movement must still carry the hearts far enough for the follower's heart to be in balance over the follower's supporting foot.)

The leader steps round the follower anticlockwise, at the same time gently carrying the follower's heart forwards. In the final position the follower's weight is some distance in front of the follower's foot. The follower could not be in this position unless supported by the leader. Even here, both torsos remain vertical. There is an optical illusion that makes the couple appear to be forming an A shape with their bodies, but that is not the case in reality. (see Dancing in a Close Hold p174)

Decorations

Everything the leader does with his or her feet beyond the minimum required to prevent the heart from falling on the floor is a decoration. Any movement the leader makes with his or her feet that interferes with the relationship between the two hearts should be abandoned, no matter how decorative it might be.

Some unskilled followers, making the mistake of thinking that the follower's role is passive, perhaps even secondary to the leaders, feel a great urge to decorate from the very start. Tempting as this is (and I succumbed to that temptation myself in the early days), it is better not to give in to it, and to concentrate on acquiring the skills of following flawlessly.

That is not to say that followers should never decorate – far from it. As one Golden Age dancer said to me, decorations are how the woman seduces the man. However, the follower's decorations only become seductive to the leader when the follower has already acquired a high level of skill, and understands the role that decorations play in the dance. If a follower attempts to decorate without that understanding, then the follower does not seduce the leader, but rather annoys and infuriates him or her.

When a couple is dancing, the leader takes responsibility for the follower's safety. The leader is the one who must constantly be aware of the other couples on the dance floor and the need to avoid collisions

The follower has given up responsibility for her or his own safety to the leader. The follower has no way of knowing whether the leader is leading a certain movement because it seems pleasing at that moment or because the leader is trying to get the couple away from a potentially unpleasant collision.

If the follower does any kind of decoration that blocks the movement across the floor that the leader was leading, then the follower may be endangering them both by increasing the chance of a collision with another couple – something that should always be avoided. If the follower decides to hold the couple still and perform some decoration, the follower may be holding up the flow of the dance floor, annoying not just the leader, but all the other couples on the floor as well.

Once the follower has achieved a high enough level in all the technical skills, the follower will start to acquire a sense of how it is possible to decorate without interrupting the dance or annoying other dancers.

My advice to followers who want to decorate is that they should learn to lead. Sometimes the desire to decorate comes from a frustrated desire to lead, or to take control in the dance. Our society, though in many ways much more liberal than that of Buenos Aires in the Golden Age, tends to reinforce the idea that men only lead, and women only follow. This is the complete antithesis of the reality of Tango in the Golden Age. Anyone interested in Tango – all men, and any women who cared to – learned to follow first and then to lead. No one was expected to be able to become a good leader without first being a good follower. And my own experience, confirmed to me by others, is that a follower's following will improve if, after reaching a certain level of skill, that follower learns to lead.

It is not simply that leading allows a person to express another side of their personality, so they feel less pressure to do intrusive decorations when they follow. It is that a person who leads understands the leader's experience, and can sense what decorations will be attractive to the leader, and what decorations would be intrusive and unpleasant, and so should be avoided. Just as the leader's leading is improved by the personal experience of feeling what works for the follower, the follower's following is improved by feeling what works for the leader.

It is easier for the leader to decorate, because the leader is in control of the movement of the couple, and knows when there is or is not time to add a little movement of the feet. All movement of the leader's feet beyond the absolute minimum necessary to lead the follower's movement without falling over can be seen as decoration. The more skilfully a leader leads, and the more accurately the follower is following, the more attention the leader can spare to allow the feet to play. The leader must be prepared, though, at any moment to stop decorating completely if full attention is required in that instant to keep the follower safe, and to keep the movement of the hearts together and controlled.

Well-executed decorations were much enjoyed by the dancers of the Golden Age. They were another way in which the individual flesh-and-blood person in your arms could be experienced, and as such increased connection and intimacy. They allowed both the leader and the follower to express the details of their own personal musicality. They were also a compliment to the other dancer's skill. Dancing with an inexperienced dancer takes more concentration, leaving fewer possibilities to decorate well.

Dancing in a Close Hold

In the Golden Age it was normal for couples to dance in a close hold, which is to say with no space between the two bodies. Exactly what that meant depended both on local style and personal preference.

At one end of the spectrum, in the north of Buenos Aires, couples tended to move with no pressure between the two bodies, sometimes even with a little space between them. At the other end of the spectrum, in the style sometimes called 'the style of the 1950s', the pressure between the two bodies was so great that if one person could be suddenly removed the other would fall over.

Wherever in the spectrum a couple chooses to dance, dancing in a close hold without making the experience horrible for your partner is highly technically demanding. Without excellent technique there is a great danger of the close hold becoming uncomfortable.

It is vital when dancing in a close hold to present your partner with a completely upright torso. If there is even the slightest hint of a lean forwards, then when the two bodies come together that lean will exert a downwards force on the partner, and this quickly becomes uncomfortable, even intolerable. Often people without excellent technique trying to get into a close hold with their partner will bring the head forwards, aiming to dance cheek to cheek. This has the effect of slightly slumping the shoulders, and even though the one doing the slumping may not even notice it has happened, the one being slumped on will feel as though for the three minutes of the dance they are forced to carry all of their partner's weight around the room. In an attempt to avoid this, many people trying to dance in a close hold either push their partner away with their head, or slide to one side, getting away from the partner's weight, but also separating the hearts. In either case the result is that the attempt to get closer has in fact left them less intimate or connected with their partner than they would have been if dancing at a distance.

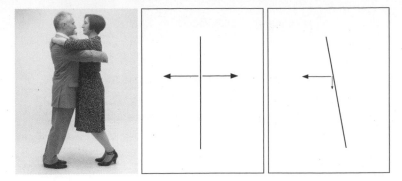

If the torsos are completely vertical then the forces between the two bodies are completely horizontal, and even if the two dancers are actually leaning on each other the position remains comfortable. If one dancer slumps the shoulders even slightly this introduces a downward component of the force between the two bodies, and the relationship can become almost intolerable to the other dancer. This is true whether the slumped person is the leader or the follower. The person slumping will almost certainly be completely unaware that they are becoming heavy and uncomfortable to dance with.

Dancing successfully in a close hold requires excellent posture, and skill in walking forwards and backwards correctly.

Trying to force a close hold when one or both of the dancers does not have good enough technique to walk well leads to compromises in the relationship that turn into habits which then become hard to break.

It is better to dance in an open hold and with a good and constant connection between the two hearts than to dance physically close but without the intimacy that good technique was designed to provide.

Everything Is Possible But Not Everything Should Be Done

Because the followers of the Golden Age waited at all times for the leader to lead each part of each movement the follower made, it was possible at any moment for the leader to lead anything that it was physically possible to do.

However, leaders knew from personal experience that some things were particularly comfortable and pleasant for the follower to do, and some things were not. A lesser consideration, though still an important one, was that some things were more aesthetically pleasing than others. In a chess game, all the movements of all of one player's pieces are possible each time it is that player's turn makes a move. That does not mean that all possible moves are equally good. A chess player will choose the next move on the basis of what brings victory closer. In Tango the leader leads the next move on the basis of what will feel best to the follower, what expresses the music most fully, what is most aesthetically pleasing, and what makes best use of the space available on the dance floor.

On the most basic level this meant never leading a movement that would result in a collision with another couple on the dance floor. That is always unpleasant for everyone concerned – sometimes actually physically dangerous, as anyone who has been kicked by someone wearing a stiletto heel will know. I marvelled many times at the ability of dancers from the Golden Age to move through tightly packed dance floors, often performing apparently complex figures, yet never bumping into anyone.

Suiting the movement to the space available is a very important skill for the leader. No matter how much a leader may want to lead a certain movement at a particular moment, if doing so would inconvenience other people on the dance floor then it simply should not be done. Tango requires respect – respect for one's partner and respect for the other people on the dance floor.

But the leader also needed to acquire a sense of what would be pleasing to the follower. It was not enough just to learn the language of Tango. A leader was expected to learn to be articulate and graceful in using that language. This skill was learned by following – not just for the nine months it usually took for a man to become a good enough follower to be allowed to try leading in the práctica, or for the three years it usually took for a man to become a good enough leader to be allowed to go to a milonga and dance with a woman. Men continued to go to the práctica to dance, to experiment, and to experience what it was like to be led through the movements they created no matter how long they had been dancing.

On several occasions I saw men who had learned in the Golden Age and continued to practise together, trying out new choreographic shapes. They were never timid in telling each other if a new move didn't come up to their standards — or in learning a new move if it did.

A leader who follows on a regular basis learns from experience what is and is not pleasant for the follower.

STAGE DANCE AND TANGO

The first evidence of Tango being danced on stage comes from the Yiddish Theatre in Buenos Aires in the 1890s. Several years before the start of Tangomania, Tango was being danced on stage in the cabarets of Montmartre, and in London a Tango couple had auditioned for a West End producer, who felt the dance was too risqué for the London stage – though by 1914, London theatres were filled with shows with the word 'Tango' in the title.

Couples from Argentina travelled to Europe and America to perform. At home there were a variety of opportunities to perform professionally in theatres and with orchestras.

In the prácticas men would give demonstrations, and sometimes those demonstrations would be of steps the men did not consider suitable for the social dance floor – fantasy steps, or *fantasía*. They enjoyed the challenge of pushing themselves to the limits, while still respecting the fact that some of the combinations possible in the Tango would be dangerous and antisocial in a milonga, and should be reserved for suitable occasions.

People who were dancing Tango professionally around the end of the Golden Age say that Tango stage choreography as we know it began in the mid-1950s. Before then, professional Tango couples were all highly skilled social dancers. They would improvise when they performed on stage, perhaps using some pre-planned figures that they could introduce at certain points.

In the 1960s and 1970s there continued to be an audience for Tango shows, in Buenos Aires and abroad. However, there was no longer a pool of young social dancers that producers of Tango shows could draw on. They began to hire dancers from other backgrounds and gave them Tango-inspired choreographies that they could perform even without knowing how to dance the Tango. For the first time it was possible for someone to become a famous Tango dancer without having ever danced in a práctica or a milonga.

When Claudio Segovia and Hector Orezzoli created the show *Tango Argentino* they chose to use a mixture of professional dancers, some of whom had danced socially in the Golden Age, and some who were too young to have had that experience. To help the younger dancers, they hired great social dancers to teach them, so they could convey something of the essence of Tango in their performances, rather than simply performing choreographies. This was one of the reasons for the great success of the show.

As might be expected, today there are many different approaches to the art of Stage Tango. At one end of the spectrum there are those whose interest in Tango began with the social dance, who see performance as a means of expressing something about the essence of Tango in a way that makes it visible and attractive to an audience, and for whom being true to the Tango is an important part of everything they do. At the other end of the spectrum are those who have come to Tango from a background in other styles of stage dance. (In Buenos Aires these dancers often come from Contemporary Dance or from the tradition known as 'Folkloro'.) Performance and entertainment are their goal, and

Tango choreography their vehicle. Their attraction to Tango may sometimes be strong enough for them to learn something about the social dance, but they may not specialise in it, or be interested in it.

The Difference Between Social Dance and Stage Dance

Social dance and stage dance are two different skills. What differentiates them is intention and purpose.

The object of stage dance is to entertain the audience. The dancers may be performing a choreography that is inspired by social dance, or may even be improvising, but the intention and purpose is to entertain people who are watching.

Social dancers may like to be watched. They may even dance better if they know someone is watching them. But the intention and purpose of social dance is to give pleasure to the person you are dancing with, and nothing else really matters.

Stage dancers generally perform choreographies. This does not have to be the case, but usually is. It is easier to impress the general audience on a regular, reliable basis by performing a prearranged choreography, designed to fit with a specific piece of music. The performer feels safer and more in control in the high-pressure arena.

Social dancers thrive on the communication generated by improvised dance, inspired by the partner and the music, unpredictable and ever changing.

Competitive dance, like stage dance, is designed for an audience – in this case the judges. The aim of each dancer is to impress the judges, and the priority is to perform movements that will catch their eye, whether or not they are pleasant to dance. Competitive dancers may try to predict the judges' taste by emulating previous champions, even if that means dancing things they might not otherwise choose to dance.

Again, competitors generally perform choreographies. The aim is not to create the spontaneous communication of an improvised social dance, but to create a performance that looks good and is entertaining.

Stage dancing is a wonderful thing, and gives pleasure to many people. Competitions can also be extremely enjoyable. Neither a stage performance nor a performance in a competition is the same as a social dance, even if the performances are versions of social dances. Not all stage dancers or competitive dancers have the skills required to dance well on the social dance floor. Not all social dancers have the skills required to dance well on the stage. One thing is not better than the other, but it is important to realise that they are different, and to suit the way one chooses to dance to the setting.

On the social dance floor it would be an insult to my partner to dance only for myself, or to dance for the people who are watching. If I have agreed to dance with someone, then it is my responsibility actually to dance *with* that person (not just to dance in front of and at the same time as them), and to dance in the way that will give my partner the most enjoyment from the experience. Getting involved with my own choreography or thinking about how I look to other people is fine, as long as it is not done at the expense of the person I am dancing with. That would be rude and disrespectful. To the dancers of the Golden Age it would have been inexcusable.

PART IV

Tango Music for the Dancer

FINDING TANGO DANCE MUSIC

The newcomer to Tango tends to assume that all Tango music is suitable for dancing. Indeed, in one sense all music can be danced to. A person or a couple can move to anything that provides some kind of rhythm, whether it is music, the sound of a clock ticking, or even the sound of industrial machinery or of traffic in the street. Any kind of sound can be used to create a choreography. There does not even need to be a predictable rhythm, as in a choreography the dancers will be familiar with the order of the sounds, and of the movements they will be doing to them. And if two dancers are both very familiar with a piece of music, they may be able to improvise to it, no matter how unpredictable it seems to someone who does not already know it, and they may find the same quality that makes the music unpredictable on first hearing to be inspiring.

In Tango a social dance is always improvised. Two people who may never have met before will be dancing an unplanned combination of movements. And they will be doing it to music that one or both of them may never have heard before.

In order to make this possible, it is advisable for social dance music to have certain characteristics. It needs to have a certain level of rhythmic predictability. That is not to say that it needs to be 'strict tempo' – certainly not for Tango! Different pieces of Tango music move at different speeds, and have different rhythmic qualities. What is needed is consistency through the piece of music, so the dancer who does not know that particular recording is not caught out.

On a more subtle level, Tango dance music needs to be music that invites the kind of movements that are Tango. Less skilful dancers tend to dance in the same way to any music, whatever it may be, and often like to dance to music that is very varied, perhaps spanning a variety of different genres. As skill and knowledge increase, dancers become more sensitive to the differences between styles of music, and between particular pieces. They appreciate more subtle distinctions that the novice may miss. And their dancing is formed by the music, so that different music creates a different dance.

For this reason experienced Tango dancers tend to favour music that was created by the musicians who played with dancers in mind. The easiest way to get this kind of music is to look for music recorded during the Golden Age by orchestras that specialised in dance music. That is not to say there is no modern music designed for dancing. However, the beginner looking for reliable dance music recordings will stand a better chance of finding them by sticking to the Golden Age.

Not all music recorded in the Golden Age was intended to be dance music, and it is helpful to bear that in mind. Some was intended for the stage or concert platform. And some orchestras recorded both dance music and music they did not expect to be danced to. Record labels occasionally have difficulty distinguishing between the different styles of recording in their catalogue, meaning that even CDs that claim to be filled with dance music may sometimes contain music that experienced Tango dancers would choose not to dance.

It is hard to recommend specific CDs, as record labels frequently delete, repackage or reformat items in their Tango collections, meaning that content and quality are unpredictable. Instead I shall highlight a number of orchestras popular with dancers both in the Golden Age and today.

There were many more orchestras playing in the Golden Age. Before good quality amplification that allowed recordings to be played, all milongas had live music. Not all orchestras had the opportunity to record, but many did. It is only possible here to list a few of the greats. (The music pages at www.totaltango.com give more information.)

Biagi

Pianist Rodolfo Biagi played a huge part in the early success of Juan D'Arienzo's orchestra before leaving to form his own. Biagi's style is the most pared down and economical of all the Golden Age Tango orchestras, making the rhythm easy to pick out. In the instrumental recordings it lacks something in lyricism compared to other orchestras of the period. The recordings with vocals have a fuller sound.

Caló

So many members of *bandoneonista* Miguel Caló's orchestra in the 1940s went on to have successful careers leading their own orchestras that it is often referred to as the 'Orchestra of the Stars'. Caló's style is smooth, rich and lyrical.

Canaro

Although violinist Francisco Canaro recorded a great deal of wonderful dance music throughout the course of his long career, it is necessary to take some care in selecting from his vast catalogue. Canaro was one of the pioneers of stage and concert Tango music, making some experiments even around the time of Tangomania in Europe. It is always advisable to listen to a Canaro CD before buying it, no matter what the period of the recordings, to be sure of what you are getting.

D'Agostino

Pianist Angel D'Agostino has the distinction of being one of the few major orchestra leaders to have been considered a good dancer himself. His style is like a very dry white wine. It may not be instantly appealing to the uninitiated, but the subtlety and elegance is much appreciated by connoisseurs.

D'Arienzo

Juan D'Arienzo is often credited with kicking off the Golden Age in Buenos Aires. Certainly his music has been a consistent favourite with dancers, ever since his first recordings, made in 1935. D'Arienzo specialised in clean, clear dance music and all his recordings were made in a style very suitable for social dance. His career lasted into the early 1970s, meaning that some of the later recordings were made in stereo, and with more sophisticated recording technology than the Golden Age could offer, giving them a fuller sound.

De Angelis

Pianist Alfredo De Angelis created a unique sound, characterised by sweeping violins, and is most loved for his luscious valses. His most reliable recordings are from the 1940s, with some excellent ones from the early 1950s, but as time went by the style gradually became less attractive to dance.

De Caro

Julio De Caro's orchestra was enormously influential, and played a large part in creating the musical sophistication that characterises Tango of the Golden Age. The ground-breaking recordings of the late 1920s and early 1930s are danceable for music of that period, and the last recordings, made in the early 1950s, are fascinating and beautiful, as improved recording quality allows the listener to fully appreciate the complexity and innovative quality of some of the arrangements. Some recordings made in the 1930s and 1940s are not aimed at the dance floor, though those that are can be excellent.

Di Sarli

Pianist Carlos Di Sarli produced disciplined, elegant dance music. Although he first recorded in the 1920s, the recordings most popular with dancers are those made in the 1940s and 1950s. The recordings from the 1950s are slower and smoother, while those from the 1940s have a more cheerful energy.

Laurenz

Pedro Laurenz was an enormously gifted bandoneon player and composer who worked with De Caro during the great period of innovation. His own orchestra in the late 1930s and 1940s has a distinctive, powerful sound.

Pugliese

Osvaldo Pugliese produced intense, muscular dance music, much loved by the dancers in southern Buenos Aires during the Golden Age. His recordings from the 1940s are challenging, but very danceable. Later recordings start to push at the boundaries of dance music, and from the 1960s onwards little is aimed at the dance floor. His performance in the Teatro Colón in Buenos Aires – one of the world's leading opera houses – in 1985 was a landmark moment in the new Argentina that emerged after the return to democracy in 1983.

Tanturi

Ricardo Tanturi's orchestra is a solid staple of Tango dance music, whether with the personable Alberto Castillo singing in the early 1940s, or the more soulful Enrique Campos later in the decade.

Troilo

Anibal Troilo is considered by some to be the best bandoneon player ever to record. His orchestra was extremely popular. The most attractive recordings for the dancer are those made in the early 1940s, when the arrangements were challenging and innovative, while still being completely danceable. Later recordings, often featuring exceptional singers, are still of a very high quality, but not quite as focused on the dance floor.

PART V
In Conclusion

THE EXPERIENCE OF THE MAJORITY

In trying to explain the story of Tango in the Golden Age in a book, inevitably I have had to make some simplifications and generalisations. Whatever statement any person may make about Tango, it would have been possible to find someone who had been dancing in the Golden Age who would have disagreed with it. Sometimes that disagreement would amount to nothing more than vocabulary, and closer examination would show that what was being described differently was actually the same thing. But with no ultimate authority to decide that one thing was right and another wrong, Tango inevitably had its real differences as well.

What I have tried to do, though, is find the common ground that united all Tango dancers, and made Tango one dance, rather than several different ones. And I have tried to explain the common experience of the majority of Tango dancers, as far as I can understand what that was.

Of course, common experience of the majority is not the experience of every individual. In particular I have talked a great deal about young men wanting to use Tango as a way of meeting women. While the overwhelming majority of men I spoke to in Buenos Aires learned to dance the Tango for that reason, obviously there were some who did not. Occasionally I met men who had begun to dance, perhaps when they were as young as eight years old, because they loved the music and felt impelled to dance it. Only later did they discover how socially useful the dance could be. And it is undoubtedly true that there were gay men who went to the prácticas in order to dance with other men, and who had no personal interest in going to milongas to dance with women.

Certainly the preferences of the women who danced the Tango exerted a powerful force on the evolution of the dance – they were the one authority that enforced high standards. Undoubtedly women contributed directly as well. Certainly there were gay men in the prácticas who also made a contribution. Certainly there was input from all the many different ethnic groups that made up the unique cocktail of Buenos Aires. I firmly believe, though, that Tango would not have become the dance it did had not the majority of the people who were creating it been men who found themselves in a world without enough women, and who were forced to make the best they could of an environment that was not quite how they wished it to be. That is why I have focused on that part of the Buenos Aires experience – the experience of the majority of people who danced Tango in Buenos Aires before the end of the Golden Age in 1955.

THE MEANING OF TANGO

When the title of this book was first suggested to me, I was a little nervous. How could anyone dare to write a book called *The Meaning of Tango*? With any creative form, people bring to it their own meanings, and find their own individual meanings in it.

But as I thought about it, I realised that even though each individual person I met who had danced the Tango in the 1940s and 1950s had their own very personal experience, underlying that was a unifying sense of what was important, of the purpose of the dance, and the place it held in their lives.

To understand their dance, and to learn to dance it in the way they did, it is necessary to understand what Tango meant to them, on many different levels.

My intention in this book has been to explain why Tango evolved the way that it did, and how the people who created it understood it. Tango is different from any other social dance I have ever experienced. Choreographically it offers wider and richer possibilities. And on the emotional level it offers an investigation of the nature of human relationships, of the meaning of intimacy, and of what it is to be human and a social creature in a world that is often lonely and isolating. The great choreographic possibilities of Tango spring from the intimate connection between the two people dancing it.

My dear friends who learned to dance in the Golden Age might raise an eyebrow to hear me say that. They would prefer to say, 'Improvisando', where I might say, 'A meditation performed by two who become one, united at the heart, seeking stillness through motion.' They would say, 'Manteniendo la relación entre los dos cuerpos' (maintaining the relationship between the two bodies), where I would say, 'Keeping the hearts perfectly united at all times.' But they would also say, quietly, so as not to be overheard and perhaps misunderstood, that dancing Tango is like being in love for three minutes.

I am profoundly grateful to them for their generosity in sharing the Tango with me, and hope I have managed to share with you a little of what they gave me.

APPENDIX 1: CLOTHES AND SHOES FOR THE DANCER

Clothes for Dancing Tango

Tango is an urban dance, not a folk dance, and so it has no 'costume'. Through all of its history, Tango has been something that people did when they went out for an evening's entertainment, and in each era people have worn their best and most fashionable clothes to dance the Tango.

In the early years of the twentieth-century, working men in Buenos Aires often wore black jackets, sometimes with a white trim, with striped grey trousers, a white scarf tied at the neck and a black hat. Photographs of early Tango often show men dressed in that manner – not because it was what they dressed up in to go dancing, but because it was what they wore every day.

During Tangomania, fashions in Europe changed to accommodate the passion for dance. Corsets became more flexible or were abandoned, skirts became softer, with the appearance of wrap skirts, tulip skirts and double layered 'lampshade' skirts, where a shorter skirt was worn over a wrap skirt, or even ankle-length divided skirts or bloomers. High stiff collars disappeared, as did wide brims on women's hats and sweeping horizontal feathers. If feathers were worn at all, they were worn vertically so as not to get into the partner's eyes. Perhaps these changes would have happened anyway, but Tangomania in Paris, fashion capital of the world at this time, certainly contributed a new urgency.

After the First World War the French government put restrictions on the employment of foreign performers, with the aim of providing work for French artists. Foreign artists were only allowed to perform as speciality acts in their own national costume. There was no national costume in Argentina, and no costume for dancing or playing the

Tango, so this gave Tango artists something of a problem. The solution they hit upon was to dress as gauchos – the legendary horsemen of the Pampas. To anyone in Argentina, nothing would have looked quite as absurd as Tango artists dressed as gauchos. Gauchos did not dance the Tango. Tango was the culture of Buenos Aires, a modern capital city, while the gauchos lived in the countryside, and had their own quite different music and dance, which belongs to the tradition known as 'Folklore'. But outside Argentina the look caught on. Valentino dressed as a gaucho to dance his famous Tango in *The Four Horsemen of the Apocalypse*, and a cliché was born.

During the Golden Age of Tango a well-dressed, fashionable man wore a suit, so that is what men wore when they danced. The period saw many changes in women's fashions, from the loose sensuality of 1930s Hollywood-inspired gowns, to the clean lines of the 1940s and the sophisticated elegance of the New Look. Of course, both men and women would choose from the fashions of the day clothes in which they felt comfortable dancing.

The success of the show *Tango Argentino* around the world created a fashion for Tango dancers outside Buenos Aires to dress in black, as the costumes for the show were shades of black, grey and silver. While dancers in Buenos Aires might occasionally have worn black, generally in a milonga they wore the same colourful clothes they would have worn to go to a party.

The Tango Renaissance has brought people from many different backgrounds and with many different aesthetic ideals into the Tango, so today it is common to see on the same dance floor a man in a well-fitting suit or a woman in an elegant dress, and another in jeans.

In the 1990s I remember talking to a man who had danced in the Golden Age, who for personal reasons had only recently returned to dancing. While he had been away from the Tango the new generation of dancers had begun going to milongas frequented by the Golden Age dancers. He was astonished to see young men going dancing in jeans and trainers or sports shoes. He felt if a man didn't go to a milonga with his shoes shined to perfection and in his best clothes, it was, and he said this with great force, *'¡Una falta de respeto a la mujer!'* – an insult to the woman.

Certainly, when dancing Tango one is in close proximity with another person, and some things are never permissible. Common sense should suggest avoiding raw onions before going dancing, for example, although unfortunately this is something that sometimes needs to be pointed out in today's Tango scene.

Personal hygiene was something that dancers from the Golden Age were absolutely meticulous about, without exception. Sadly I know dancers in Europe who don't get danced with because their potential partner knows the odour will stay with them – whether that is an over-strong perfume or aftershave, or something more personal. This would never have happened in Buenos Aires. And for the sake of their partners, a person who knows they perspire heavily during physical activity should bring with them several changes of clothing, or wear sufficient layers to prevent the dampness from reaching their partner's notice. There are few things worse at a dance than being clasped tightly by someone and finding your own clothes soaked with their cold sweat.

Common sense should allow any dancer to avoid all these pitfalls – common sense and respect for the people with whom one is going to be dancing. Without respect for one's partner one can never be a good Tango dancer.

Provided that one takes one's partner's comfort into consideration, pretty much anything goes in the modern Tango scene, just as it does elsewhere in our culture. Always choose clothes you can move in easily. Trying to dance while also trying to hold in place a skimpy top can be unsettling, and a tight skirt can restrict movement, for example.

Classes tend to be informal, with ease of movement being the most important thing, so dressing for comfort when going to a class is always appropriate. If a dance follows the class, however, then one should dress with the dance in mind. When hoping to dance for the first time with someone you don't know, it is helpful to remember that first impressions count for a lot. The way you dress does show your respect for the person you plan to hold in your arms. It also shows your respect for yourself. As one Argentinian friend said to me, the dance begins not when you walk up to your partner, but when you stand in your home planning what you are going to wear.

Shoes

The ideal shoe for dancing the Tango has a smooth sole, allowing the foot to turn easily. While Ballroom dancers use suede soles, which can be brushed up to give more grip on a slippery floor, Tango dancers favour leather. If a dancer stands with the correct posture for Tango, then the dancer's weight is directly over the balls of the toes, and unless a floor is dangerously slippery, the dancer should be able to feel comfortably balanced without the need of extra grip. Trainers, sports shoes, or other shoes that are designed to have a great deal of grip on the floor, can be dangerous as they prevent turning, forcing the dancer to twist the leg instead and putting unnatural pressure on the joints, which over time could lead to injury.

Ordinary men's outdoor shoes in the traditional English style often have a stiff sole with a lip extending beyond the edge of the foot, and this should be avoided if possible. A thin sole which does not extend beyond the upper is much better as it makes the shoe lighter and easier to dance in. Similarly, platform shoes and wedge heels should be avoided, as they tend to make a shoe inflexible.

The shoe must have a flexible sole to allow the foot to extend backwards correctly, with the toes placed flat on the floor while the rest of the foot is in line with the lower leg.

It is also important that the shoe provides good support, and stays securely on the foot, particularly, again, when stepping back. If the heel of the shoe falls away from the foot when the dancer steps back it will be impossible to dance comfortably or well. For this reason lace-up shoes, or shoes with straps at the ankle or high on the arch, tend to be preferred. Slingback heels offer no support, and court shoes or other shoes without straps tend to fall away from the heel when walking backwards in the Tango way, unless they are uncomfortably tight.

A leader needs a heel of roughly the normal height of a man's shoe, though some prefer a slightly higher heel. A heel that is too high results in a weak, unclear lead. A follower should generally be in a higher heel, as the heel provides support to the foot when walking backwards. Also, it is important for the follower to be able to allow the heel to touch the floor (while not actually putting any weight on it) as this allows the leg to rest and relax correctly. An experienced follower, who has the correct tone in the leg, will be able to follow in shoes with a low heel and still allow the heel to rest on the floor, but for the inexperienced follower the result of dancing in a heel that is too low is that they will dance constantly on their toes. It is almost impossible to get the correct tonic relaxation in the leg when constantly standing on the toes. Some dancers like to practise in low-heeled shoes. Of course, comfort is vital – no one can dance well if their feet hurt! – but it will be more difficult for a follower to acquire the technique of the Golden Age dancers if the follower dances or practises in low-heeled shoes.

APPENDIX 2: SOME TANGO TERMS EXPLAINED

Cabezeo

In the milongas of Buenos Aires it is not considered polite to go up to someone and ask them to dance, as it puts pressure on the person who is asked to say yes even if they would prefer not to dance, and it puts the person asking at risk of losing face if the person asked does say no. If a person wants to dance with someone, that person tries to catch the other person's eye. Once eye contact has been made, and the agreement to dance has been reached, the leader goes to the follower's table and only then does the follower stand.

Because it is the leader who goes to the follower once the agreement has been made, it is easy to get the impression that it is the leader that always does the asking. In reality the *cabezeo* is completely fair and equal, as a leader cannot catch a follower's eye if the follower chooses not to dance, and the follower can initiate eye contact as easily as the leader can.

Making eye contact with someone across the room is easier when the music is arranged in *tandas*, as the dance floor clears at regular intervals, allowing all dancers the opportunity of making eye contact with each other.

Canyengue

Canyengue is a word used by people in Buenos Aires who are not part of the Tango community to refer to that indefinable quality that gives Tango its character.

People who study Tango music use the word Canyengue to refer to the early Tango style (see *'Dos por Cuatro'*). The word has long been associated by historians of Tango with the style of dance from that period. It is also sometimes used as though it applied to a style from the

Golden Age (though if it ever did apply to a style danced in the Golden Age, I have never been able to identify what that style was or find anyone who danced it at that time).

As dancers of the Tango Renaissance came to Buenos Aires looking for authentic Tango, they began asking dancers to show them Canyengue, as they had heard the word used as the name of a Tango style. Some dancers tried to show people the dance they remembered seeing people who had danced in the 1910s and 1920s doing, which led other dancers to begin developing their own, very individual, and often very appealing, interpretations in what they felt a Canyengue style might be. In the 1990s these interpretations were developed into a new style of Tango, also called Canyengue, that was very fashionable for a while. There is little evidence to suggest that this new style bears much resemblance to the Tango as it was danced in the early years of the twentieth century, though it is charming, and continues to be popular with some dancers.

Compadrito

The *compadres* were the dangerous tough guys of Buenos Aires in the late nineteenth and early twentieth centuries. *Compadrito* is a diminutive of *compadre*, and was used to describe the streetwise *porteño* who might have liked to think he was a *compadre*, but who did not have quite such high status.

Conventillo

A tenement block, where many people lived in one building. These were home to immigrants and the poor.

Cortina

Cortina, or curtain, is the term used for a piece of non-dance music used to separate the *tandas* at a milonga. It is the signal for all the couples on the dance floor to return to their places as one kind of music ends and another kind begins.

Dos por Cuatro

Tango is often referred to in Buenos Aires as *dos por cuatro* (literally 'two by four') referring to the time signature used for early Tango – 2/4, or two crotchets (quarter notes) to the bar (measure). *Dos por cuatro* Tango was played with a lilting heartbeat rhythm. Dividing each bar into eight equal parts, that rhythm is:

1 2 3 **4 5** 6 **7** 8
or
1 2 3 **4 5 6 7** 8

Musicologists in Buenos Aires generally refer to early Tango music in the *dos por cuatro* rhythm as *canyengue*.

By 1920 that rhythm had completely disappeared from the Tango, to be replaced by the square rhythm of mature Tango:

1 2 **3** 4 **5** 6 **7** 8

where emphasis on the '4' is used only occasionally for effect.

The *dos por cuatro* rhythm reappeared in Milonga in the 1930s, with a jazzy variant of it also appearing in Tango Nuevo.

Estilo Milonguero

A style of Tango developed in the 1990s, based on the style of Tango danced in certain parts of central and southern Buenos Aires in the 1950s. See *Milonguero*.

Golden Age of Tango

The Golden Age of Tango is the period between 1935 and 1955 – usually referred to in Buenos Aires as the decade of the 1940s, even though it was twenty years long. It is the period when all the branches of Tango were in the most perfect harmony, and the highest levels of achievement were reached in all of them.

Gotan

Tango. In *Lunfardo* it is common to reverse the order of syllables in a word.

Lunfardo

It is said that Buenos Aires is a city of French architecture inhabited by Italians who speak Spanish and wish they were English. Lunfardo, the dialect or argot of the *porteños*, reflects the cultural diversity of the city. It contains many words of Italian origin (some of them nineteenth-century slang words in Italy), though all the different communities that arrived in Buenos Aires left their mark on it. It is also common to hear back slang, where the order of syllables in a word is reversed – *Gotan* for Tango, for example.

Milonga

The word 'milonga' can be confusing, because it has several different meanings.

Milonga first appears as the name of a type of folk-song. Its function is as a carrier of lyrics, and it was popular with improvising singers. Like the kind of blues that often begins, 'I woke up this morning . . .' there is a standard conventional harmonic and rhythmic base over which lyrics are chanted, in an almost tuneless way. All folk milongas have fundamentally the same chanting tune, so it would be almost impossible to distinguish one from another without hearing the lyrics.

Before the all-conquering dominance of Tango in Buenos Aires, folk music was the most popular music in the city, and folk singers were some of the biggest stars Buenos Aires produced. Milongas were very popular, and showed off the singer's virtuosity with lyrics, especially when the singer improvised. People would go to hear folk singers, and would say that they were going to hear a milonga, and then going to a milonga, so gradually milonga became a word meaning a place where one went to hear folk music.

Other styles of folk music would also be played at these milongas. While today the 'Folklore' community in Argentina does not dance to the folk milonga – which is logical, as its function is to carry lyrics, so it is to be listened to, not danced to – other folk-music styles have exciting dances that became very popular. Even the milongas may at one time have been danced (or possibly, as they were so popular, the word may have been used as an umbrella term for any music and dance favoured by the *compadritos*). Gradually the word milonga came to mean a place where one went to dance. This sense of the word is still used in Buenos Aires today. The place where one goes to dance Tango is known as a milonga.

In his autobiography, Francisco Canaro claimed that it was he who invented the term 'tango milonga' in 1917 to describe a tango specifically designed for dancing. Certainly the term was in common use before the end of the First World War, and was being used in Europe in the 1920s to refer to the new 4/8 Tango rhythm being brought over by Tango orchestras touring Europe at that time. The emergence of two new forms of Tango music, tango canción (sung tangos) and tango fantasía (symphonic tangos designed for the concert platform), made it necessary to specify which recordings were designed for dancing. Tango milonga, then, was not in itself an innovation, but a new label given to what would previously have been simply called Tango.

In 1932 the songwriting team of Homero Manzi and Sebastian Piana started an experiment that led to the invention of the Milonga, the third pillar of the Tango Trinity (Tango, Milonga and Vals), as Tango dancers know it today. Manzi wanted to write a lyric for a milonga, the still-popular folk-song style. Piana was not interested because he felt that as a composer a milonga left him with nothing to do. The tune, harmonic structure and style were all laid down by convention. So they agreed they would try something new. Manzi would write his lyric, but Piana would set it creating a new melody and harmonic structure, more in the style of a tango. The result was the song *Milonga Sentimental*, which immediately became a huge hit. Manzi and Piana instantly set about experimenting further with their discovery, turning out several of the new kind of milonga song, with varying degrees of success.

Other composers and performers quickly took up the new idea. The Tango had been slowing down through the 1920s and early 1930s, and artists like Canaro saw in this new Milonga the opportunity to play something more like the dance tangos of the early years of their careers, as well as playing the more modern slow tangos. Other artists took the traditional folk milonga tune and lyrics and placed them over Tango-inspired arrangements.

This burst of creativity produced something new – something called a milonga, but which could exist as an instrumental, without lyrics, and was designed for dancing. This is sometimes called *milonga ciudadana* (city milonga), to distinguish it from the still popular *milonga surena* or *campera*, southern or country milonga, as the folk style is sometimes called today. To Tango dancers, though, *milonga ciudadana* is just Milonga, and born just as the Golden Age of Tango was about to begin, it quickly took its place as the third pillar of the Tango Trinity.

The different meanings of milonga, then, are:

1) a folk-song form designed to carry lyrics, with a simple melody with few variations, and strict harmonic structure

2) a place where dancing of any kind is done, generally today meaning a Tango venue, where all three forms of Tango – Tango, Milonga and Vals – and in Buenos Aires frequently *Jazz* and *Tropical*, would also be danced

3) in the phrase 'tango milonga', a tango composition or recording specifically designed for dancing (as opposed to a song or concert work that was not created for dancing), generally referring to a work created around the time of transition from 2/4 to 4/8

4) the youngest member of the Tango Trinity (Tango, Milonga and Vals), invented in the 1930s. It is the playful face of Tango, usually faster than Tango, and frequently exhibiting some of the swing of the early 2/4 Tango. This is Milonga as Tango dancers think of it.

Milonguero

Milonguero literally means someone who frequents milongas. During the early years of the Tango Renaissance the word was used to mean someone who learned how to dance the Tango in Buenos Aires during the Golden Age.

The development of a style in the 1990s which was given the name 'Estilo Milonguero' led to a great deal of confusion over the use of the word. This style took its inspiration from the style of Tango danced in some parts of central and southern Buenos Aires in the 1950s. It was a reaction against the choreographically complex styles favoured by most Tango schools in Buenos Aires and elsewhere in the early years of the Tango Renaissance, and was a genuine attempt to focus on the essence of Tango. However, the name of the style implied not just that this was *one* of the ways in which Tango was danced in the Golden Age, but that it was the *only* way, reinforcing the unfounded prejudice that complex figures were a distortion of Tango with no place on the social dance floor.

Sadly, on several occasions I saw men I respected, fabulous dancers, some of whom had been dancing since the early 1940s, profoundly hurt because members of the new generation of dancers had accused them of not being the real thing – not being real Tango dancers – because they did not dance in the style called 'Estilo Milonguero'.

Ocho

Figure of eight. An ocho is a step where the leader leads the follower to make a figure of eight shape, either forwards, by alternating turning forwards steps, or backwards, alternating turning backwards steps.

Ocho Cortado

An extended forwards ocho. The follower is led to do the first step of a forwards ocho, but the turn continues, as though the follower was going to be taken into the turning walk. Before the side step has been completed the leader reverses the direction of the follower's movement, taking a side step in the opposite direction (the two side steps usually taking one beat of the music) followed by a turning forwards step. This may be repeated on the other side.

Orillero

Orillero literally means 'from the outskirts' – the *orillas*. Outside the Tango dance community in Buenos Aires the term is sometimes used as though it referred to a particular style of dance (to distinguish it from Tango de Salón). I never spoke to anyone who had danced socially in the Golden Age of Tango who referred to the style he or she danced as 'Orillero'. Whatever style they danced, everyone, without exception in my own experience, referred to what they did as Tango de Salón.

I found no evidence of what a dance style called Orillero might have been. My conclusion from the information that I managed to collect is that Orillero may in the early years of Tango have been synonymous with Canyengue – that is to say a style of Tango that was not Tango de Salón, not Tango that was danced in respectable dance halls, but an older style that was danced in the makeshift, rough-and-ready venues of the port, and perhaps other areas around the edge of the city.

Orquesta Típica

The typical Tango orchestra. The backbone of the *orquesta típica* is the sextet of two bandoneons, two violins, double bass and piano. Larger orchestras add more bandoneons, more strings, and occasionally other instruments as well.

Parada

A step in which the leader interrupts the movement of the follower's body, generally during the transfer section of a step back. The leader immobilises the follower, then generally performs some decorative movement – sometimes sandwiching the follower's front foot between the leader's feet, though many other variations are possible. *Parada* means 'stop'.

Porteño

A person or thing from Buenos Aires.

Práctica

In the Golden Age of Tango a práctica was a men's practice dance, which was also used by new Tango dancers as a place to learn the dance. Today the term is often used for a low-key social dance.

Sacada

A step in which the leader appears to knock the follower's supporting leg away. This is in fact an optical illusion – the leader uses his or her own leg as a lever under the follower's body to move the follower's torso. The follower's leg is moved by the movement of the bodies. Sacada comes from *sacar* – to take away.

Salida

The traditional first four steps of the dance. Salida means 'exit', or 'place where a journey begins', or 'going outside'. In the Tango Renaissance salida has come also to mean the 'Eight Step Basic' that is taught in many Tango classes. In the Golden Age, each area of Buenos Aires, sometimes even to the level of each práctica, had its own form of the salida. Experienced dancers could tell where a leader came from by the way he led the first four steps.

It is interesting to note that the 'Eight Step Basic' was not the salida of any part of Buenos Aires in the Golden Age. (It seems to have been invented by Tango teachers in the 1980s.) While the two halves of the step both existed in every part of the city, and the 'Normal Resolution' that finishes the step was very common, the first half of the step, up to the cross, was surprisingly rarely used, and then only when useful choreographically.

Salón

Salón, or Tango de Salón, is a term that can be extremely confusing.

Outside Buenos Aires it is often used to refer to any one of a number of different styles of Tango.

In my own research in Buenos Aires, I frequently asked people who had been dancing in the Golden Age what style of Tango they danced. All of them, whatever style they danced, said that they danced Tango de Salón. If I asked them to describe the style of another dancer who danced differently from them, particularly if it was a style of which they did not approve, they would find another description for it. Invariably, though, that other dancer referred to what he did as Tango de Salón.

My conclusion is that Tango de Salón refers not to a particular style of Tango, but actually to the change in the nature of Tango. The early *dos por cuatro* music and the dance that went with it were confined to the poorer parts of Buenos Aires society, enjoyed in an impromptu fashion in the patios of the *conventillos* and other places of working-class entertainment. After Tangomania raised the respectability of the dance it began the journey into dance halls and ballrooms – into the *salón*.

At the same time, the change in the rhythm of the music led to a change in the way the dance was done. This was more fundamental than a superficial stylistic change. It was the development of mature Tango.

Across the city of Buenos Aires there were many, many different choreographic styles, and yet there was an astonishing uniformity in the fundamental technique. It is this fundamental technique that defines Tango de Salón.

Confusingly, though, dancers of different choreographic styles tended to concentrate on those differences when talking about Tango to young dancers of the Tango Renaissance, identifying their own style as Tango de Salón, and therefore excluding all other styles. This led young dancers to define Tango de Salón as a style, rather than the technique that binds all Tango dancers together. This in turn led to the use of other terms such as 'Orillero' or sometimes even 'Nuevo' to separate styles that were all considered by those who created and danced them in the Golden Age to be Tango de Salón.

Sandwich

A step where the leader, having first interrupted the follower's movement, usually in a turning back step, though sometimes in a turning forwards step, then proceeds to place the feet either side of the follower's front foot, sandwiching it between the leader's own feet. The follower's movement is not interrupted by the placing of the leader's feet, but by the movement of the hearts suddenly stopping before the movement of the follower's foot can be completed.

Tanda

A *tanda* is a group of tracks by the same orchestra and in the same style. In the milongas in Buenos Aires the dance music is organised in *tandas* separated by curtain music.

Although to the inexperienced dancer the idea of playing music in *tandas* seems strange as it interrupts the dancing, in fact it is an enormous help in facilitating the working of the milonga.

Clearing the floor every ten to fifteen minutes means that no matter how crowded the dance is, it is possible for dancers to have the space to dance more complicated choreographic patterns for a minute or two before the floor fills again.

When the floor is clear it is easy to make eye contact with someone anywhere in the room. And every person in the room is free at the beginning of the *tanda*, so the situation never arises that two people want to dance with each other but whenever one is free the other is dancing.

The system also facilitates dancing with new people and increases the social fluidity of the milonga. At the *cortina* everyone will stop dancing. Each milonga will have a certain number of tracks in each *tanda*, so everyone knows how many tracks there are to go before the *cortina*. With just one or two tracks to go it is easy to agree to dance with someone you don't know, and perhaps would not otherwise dance with.

Tango Nuevo

Tango Nuevo means 'new Tango', and so has been used over the years to refer to a variety of things that once seemed new and different. It is most commonly used to refer to the style of Tango music pioneered by Astor Piazzolla in the 1970s and 1980s. This was a period when there was very little dancing, and so no real market for Tango aimed at the dance floor. Piazzolla, who had grown up in New York surrounded by Jazz (and who had expressed a desire to create Tango music that could not be danced to), used the term to refer to the Tango-Jazz fusion music he was experimenting with – a style of music that proved to be very accessible to those with no experience of the Tango tradition. It was also popular with stage dancers, who ironically found that they could create interesting choreographies to the music not designed for dancing.

Piazzolla's Tango Nuevo continues to influence musicians both inside and outside the Tango world almost two decades after his death.

Recently the term Tango Nuevo has been applied to a style of Tango dance using complicated choreographic ideas, although in practice the choreographic ideas used in this style have been in existence since the Golden Age, and perhaps earlier.

Vals

Tango in waltz time. When danced with Tango steps it is sometimes referred to as *Vals Cruzado* (Vals with the cross). Even in the Golden Age, in some parts of Buenos Aires people still danced Viennese Waltz to Vals music, or a few bars of Viennese Waltz mixed in with *Vals Cruzado*. Vals is the joyful face of Tango, and is one of the three parts of the Tango Trinity – Tango, Vals and Milonga. The three together give Tango its fully rounded personality.

ACKNOWLEDGEMENTS

So many people have been a vital part of my investigation of Tango over the years that it is impossible to thank everyone, and I apologise to those that I do not mention by name. I will never forget the contribution you made to my life and my dancing. Of the many teachers who have helped me, I must particularly thank Rodolfo Dinzel, Mingo and Esther Pugliese, and the great Eduardo Arquimbau. And of the friends who tore their heart from their body and gave it to me when they saw that I had a genuine desire to understand, the dearest of all are Juan Bruno, Alcibiades, and Manolo Salvador.

And I must not forget the friends in London without whom the journey would never have begun, Danny Evans, Diana Syrat, Dan Altman, Jane Whelan and Peter Ryan — and Barry Jones, without whom the journey would not have continued.

I must also thank my agent Shelley Power for believing in this book from the start, and Tom Bromley at Portico for encouraging me to change the simple beginners' book I originally envisaged into the one that I wanted to write.

Christine Denniston

Photographs on pages 12, 13, 16, 20, 26, 63
Source: Archivo General de la Nación Dpto Doc Fotográficos, Argentina

Dancers in the illustrations: Christine Denniston and Barry Jones